D1319970

Driftworks

Jean-Francois Lyotard

FOREIGN AGENTS SERIES

Jim Fleming and Sylvere Lotringer, Series Editors

IN THE SHADOW OF THE SILENT MAJORITIES
Jean Baudrillard

ON THE LINE
Gilles Deleuze and Felix Guattari

DRIFTWORKS
Jean-Francois Lyotard

POPULAR DEFENSE AND ECOLOGICAL STRUGGLES
Paul Virilio

SIMULATIONS
Jean Baudrillard

THE SOCIAL FACTORY
Toni Negri and Mario Tronti

PURE WAR
Paul Virilio / Sylvere Lotringer

FORGET FOUCAULT
Jean Baudrillard

Driftworks

Jean-Francois Lyotard

Edited by Roger McKeon

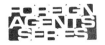

FOREIGN
AGENTS
SERIES

Semiotext(e), Inc.
522 Philosophy Hall
Columbia University
New York, New York 10027 U.S.A.

Contents

Opening by Roger McKeon 1
Adrift 9
On Theory: An Interview 19
Jewish Oedipus 35
The Connivances of Desire with the Figural 57
Notes on the Critical Function of the Work of Art 69
Gift of Organs 85
Several Silences 91
Notes on the Texts 111
Biographical Notes 113
Uncollected Works 115
Note on Translators 117

Driftworks

Jean-Francois Lyotard

Opening

The providential idler in whose hands *Driftworks* will fall may wonder why we are publishing J.-F. Lyotard in the empires of a neo-positivism one would think totally impervious to the drifter's disordering propositions. He will not have yet realized that the era of imperial Reason is coming to its end, and that he is living in the last days of man. He should know, moreover, that Lyotard's thought has been gaining ground for quite a while on a continent much less hostile to the drift than appearances would tend to indicate. Like two of the flying professor's most recent books,[1] the collection offered here was born of his encounter with America. It deals, as one will soon find out, with the correlation between the work of art and politics, the angles from which this is considered changing as time goes by. Lyotard's thought is in the plural, or, to put it more accurately, his thoughts have no singular. Their progression eludes all vigilance, they move lightly towards unguarded targets, in accordance, it seems, with no declared or undeclared finality . . . guerrilla thoughts, daughters of opportunity, ever ready to exploit the slightest irregularities of the grounds they scout and refuse to invest.

Lyotard assigns the work of art a deconstructive role. He finds in it both an instrument allowing us to *see* through the gaps of dominant ideologies, and the source from which new methods could be drawn in the struggle against the system(s). That the artist, unlike the procrastinating philosopher, precedes his time, is not a new idea, and the demystifying power of imagination was recognized long before Lyotard came on the scene, as is demonstrated *inter alia* by the scope and impact of the surrealist movement in today's world. His originality lies elsewhere; it is largely and paradoxically due to the ponderous legacy of ideas—primarily Marxism, psychoanalysis and phenomenology—against which he spends time sharpening his claws. It is no doubt significant, incidentally, that these three trends originated outside French thought and, as far as the first two are concerned, at least (which happen to be those we are mainly interested in here), that the primacy of Descartes' reasoning Ego is implicitly discredited at the outset. Be that as it may, Lyotard is certainly no orphan; his struggle against the past is waged on several fronts, and there is no shortage of opponents.

To put it very roughly, what he rejects from Marx is his inveterate Hegelianism; history has no ends, it is not made, whatever one may say, of progressive negations leading to an ideal and transparent society in which alienation would disappear. It has, indeed, demonstrated this in no uncertain terms, and Lyotard deems the Marxist ideal of reconciliation to be an ideological relic inherited from Christianity; his position nevertheless derives from Marx's attitude towards the theories of Feuerbach: "Marx understands that criticizing the *signified*—mediation as the intelligible content of reconciliation—is not sufficient: that, Feuerbach knows how to do; what must be criticized as well is the very position on which utterances are based [. . .]. Discourse can cease to edify and to plead through what it says, while continuing to be a mediator external to the mediated terms, on account of its sole position. The place where I speak from should be suspected; a discourse, be it that of anxiety, can be consoling, madness can inhabit rationality . . ."[2]

Not only is Kapital indifferent to the critique of the signified, it requires it. Another method must thus be developed, one not of theoretical critique, but of deconstruction; hence the importance granted to the work of art and to Freudian discoveries. Deconstruction is not a task for language, implying as it does not only a shift of position, but also of space, which has nothing to do with critique, in that it leaves the safe shores of the secondary process to become the producer of the other scene. The very term "deconstruction" is indicative: one can only deconstruct what has been constructed—at the expense, Lyotard argues, of desire, which Freud was clever enough to catch a glimpse of in the gaps of the secondary process. There is one certainty in this regard, namely that desire is intolerable and that all cultures aim at damming it up. The paradox is, nonetheless, that the most advanced manifestations of Western culture have tended to destroy the dikes set up against the uncontrollable thrusts of this disquieting force. Neither the processes that were at work yesterday, nor those taking place today, can, strictly speaking, be termed "critical"; we are dealing with attacks on form, changes in the positions of significance.

Who would doubt that capitalism has accelerated the obsolescence of all forms? This superannuation started long before the system came into being, however, and nothing indicates that it will not go on long after its disappearance. For desire—with which *Discours, figure* is almost wholly concerned—cannot be satisfied. Artists fascinate Lyotard in that, unlike the common herd, they have the courage (but not always the strength, as more than one tragic fate reminds us) to let this desire that their contemporaries repress manifest itself. The contribution of art cannot be reduced to a mastery of forms, as is demonstrated by the sorrowful mediocrity of some formally perfect productions, whose very perfection upholds the most firmly established and decrepit of orders; no one can ever pretend to master desire, the manifestations of which Lyotard takes to be so many intimations of truth. It is perhaps superfluous to stress the importance that Freudian methodology, founded as it is on silent expectation, takes on in this regard. It should however be noted—and perhaps this is where Lyotard parts company, if not with the master of Vienna whose radical scepticism he emphasizes,[3] at least with a number of his epigones, convinced of their hold over truth—that, naked or not, thruth never manifests itself where it is expected, no doubt because it is always a step ahead of knowledge.

The essays you are about to read were written shortly after May 1968; the point, here, is not to assess the historical significance or insignificance of that turbulent spring, but to insist on its examplary nature; not only was the "revolution" totally unexpected, but the various organized forces which were then on stage immediately attempted to take the lion's share and to exploit the unexploitable: fortuity. The Communist party was bitterly accused of turning its sails to the wind and catching the last train, but it was only the most awkward and cumbersome of the laggards. History will never be serious; it had just winked and everyone hurried to speculate on the disturbance, to turn it to practical account, as if the truth of the event could be found in the senile utterances of established structures. Turbulence is history's vocation, and organized man burdened with his so-called knowledge, will never learn, to judge by his persistence in deluding himself, that he always arrives too late to train it. Lyotard would never come to the conclusion that action is useless, however; taking a leaf out of the artist's book, he considers that the deconstruction of the system cannot be carried out on the level of the secondary process and of its efficacy, but requires a receptivity always on the alert, an active passivity . . .

To replace one form of power with another is of no great interest to anyone, for, as history also shows, such an operation cannot but take place entirely within the field of the signified. Unlike the futile babble of art criticism, artists' deconstructive critique does not talk, it works. And this is also the function which Lyotard assigns to the opponents of the system: act at the right moment, unhinge the institutional forms and drop all safeguards. In short, risk going the wrong way. A tactical thought, thus, that strategy ruffles and which could not and would not give the lead.

What we must understand at this point is that if capitalism is a prime opponent, neither should the so-called "socialist" solution be spared. ("If the question is thus of knowing what really ruins bourgeois society, the answer obviously cannot be found in socialist revolution, nor does it reside in Marxism. Not only has historical 'dialectic' given the lie to speculative dialectic, but we must recognize that it is not a dialectic at all.")[4] The time wihin which Lyotard drifts is no longer that of such a simple opposition: the "system" has established itself on both sides of the 14th degree of Eastern longitude, and the fact that its modalities differ according to its situation in relation to this boundary is from now on of little importance. History, that old harlot, has seemingly undertaken to slew round the axes of opposition by ninety degrees, so that the overlap of dividing lines and parallels of latitude is becoming clearer and clearer. The real battles are no longer waged between empires; in spite of a few rear-guard skirmishes, of shows of aggressive volubility and of the common determination to invest all areas opened to ideology and new transactions by the withdrawal of the last colonial forces and the downfall of their strongholds, the true threats against the globe, those ripping open its stitches, lie elsewhere. The systems have already begun to break up from within, everything is coming to pieces, and it is hardly necessary to put a shoulder to the wheel.

Lyotard does not grieve over decadence or the decline of values; quite the contrary, he delights in them, and what he advocates, rather than a critique of Kapital, is the exarcebation of the most advanced phenomena that characterize it. Similar in this to the artist, compelled to satisfy a market more and more avid for novelty and to deconstruct all forms, one after the other, in his frantic flight from the past, the intellectual facing the system has no choice but to cover up his tracks and slip into elusiveness.

A new sophistics takes form in this drift, the eternal truth sought by the great haters of flux and temporality, the Platonists, is relegated to the attic of history. Truth is closely bound up with time, its faithful accomplice. Like the latter, it glides away and never surrenders itself. Its manifestations cannot be foreseen, it should not even be awaited, for the expectation is bound to be disappointed. This is a profoundly Jansenistic attitude, and, in spite of all appearances to the contrary, there is nothing of the atheist about Lyotard. The atheist still believes too much, makes himself a believer in non-belief, "wants to hear what the voice of the Other says, instead of being seized and dispossessed [. . .],"[5] a position much too voluntaristic, too imbued with certainty, which is "the pathos of knowledge."[6] Lyotard is a Jansenist in that he challenges all certainty. Nothing is guaranteed. Truth has its reasons that Reason knows not, it has never been reasonable, and there is no reason why history should lead to its reign. Claiming to follow the course of history would thus be senseless—in the strongest sense of the word—for history knows no true course. This doesn't mean, again, that action is unnecessary, but explains Lyotard's evolution and his progressive relinquishment of deconstruction in favor of what some would call, perhaps with more relevance that they might realize, a surrender: "impower and disseizure." Since no one can hence be the herald (or hero?) of reason, the intellectual struggling against obscurantism has no choice but to open up the field within which truth could manifest itself. Nothing says it will, but opportunity makes the thief. . .

A reason no longer produced by the monopolizing Ego of the philosopher-king, that knows no master, serves no ends and respects neither law nor religion dawns thus on the horizon of thought. The reign of active scepticism has already begun, the rule of the undecidable is coming into force, and Lyotard, the most destitute of all outcasts tramping on the most disabled of all cockleshells, has sided with them. The weapons he now proposes are those of the weak: humor, parody, description. . . , letting things and beings act, and showing how they mock all knowledge.

That the work of art should remain privileged at the very time when Lyotard turns away from its critical value, preferring to let himself be "fascinated by the factuality of a form, of an approach, of a detail, of a flow even, [so as to attempt] to convey its potential energy, to *show* the vast perspective that this trifle opens. . . ,"[7] may seem incongruous to those concerned with efficiency. The untimely scorns efficiency, however, for it is "a concept and a practice of power, counter-revolutionary in its very principle."[8] Lyotard pursues his elusive course while all the values of the West crumble around him. Rather than attempting to reconstitute the system which would allow him to muffle the deafening grindings of all the mechanisms into which time once again beguiles itself pouring its grains of sand, he maintains himself in the anxiety of the death drive. New Platonists are already rising, who would like to silence the blasphemer and make an end of indecency. But history does not repeat itself. . .

Roger McKeon

Notes

1. *Récits tremblants* & *Le mur du Pacifique*, Galilée 1977 & 1979
2. "La place de l'aliénation dans le retournement marxiste," *Dérivee à partir de Marx et Freud*, p. 87 (10/18, 1973).
3. "Apathie dans la théorie," *Rudiments païens* (10/18, 1977).
4. "Capitalisme énergumène," *Des dispositifs pulsionnels*, p. 16 (10/18, 1973).
5. "Oedipe juif," *Dérive à partir de Marx et Freud*, p. 187.
6. "Dissertation sur une inconvenance," *Rudiments païens*, p. 233
7. Foreword to *A partire da Marx e Freud* (Multhipla, Milan, 1979).

Adrift

Is an introduction to these essays really necessary? Don't they introduce themselves? Their presentation can only be a re-presentation. I shall place myself behind them, under them, and say: this is what they mean. Thus, my representation will say what they mean and what they actually say will automatically be invalidated, "absented" and considered illusory. By representing them I make them characters in an affair under my control, parts in a text which is mine and not theirs, while the opposite is true: theirs is the only text, and I who would pretend to refer the production of (and the credit for) these essays to my authorship through this representation, am in fact nothing authorized before them, nothing interesting without them. I have no secret to reveal, everything is there, exposed on the surface.

——In that case, why do you preface them?

Not to provide the key and demonstrate their unity, but rather to make them drift a little more than they seem to. What should be suspected is their apparent unity; their collection is interesting insofar as some elements remain uncollected. There is in every text a principle of displaceability (*Verschiebbarkeit*, said Freud), on account of which the written work induces other displacements here and there (within author and readers both), and can thus never be but the snapshot of a mobile, itself a referred, secondary unity, under which currents flow in all directions. By collecting texts and making them a book, one encloses them in a protective membrane and they become part of a cell which will defend its unity; my aim, in presenting the essays collected here, is to break up this unity.

What is important in a text is not what it means, but what it does and incites to do. What it does: the charge of affect it contains and transmits. What it incites to do: the metamorphoses of this potential energy into other things—other texts, but also paintings, photographs, film sequences, political actions, decisions, erotic inspirations, acts of insubordination, economic initiatives, etc. These essays conceal nothing, they do or do not contain a certain amount of force with which the reader will or will not do something; their content is not a signification but a potentiality. As a consequence, I am not in a privileged position to detect their intensity in general. I have only read them before the readers.

Driftworks in the plural, for the question is not of leaving *one* shore, but several, simultaneously; what is at work is not one current, pushing and tugging, but different drives and tractions. Nor is just one individual *embarking* here, or even a collective of individuals, but rather, as in Bosch's *Ship*, a collection of fools, each fool being an exaggerated part of the normal subject, libido cathected in such and such a sector of the body, blocked up in this or that configuration of desire, all these fragments placed next to each other (the category of *neben*!) for an aimless voyage, a collection of fragments impossible to unify for it drifts with the Ship, its very drift giving the advantage of the strongest resonance now to one *Trieb*-fool, now to another, in accordance with the diversity of the times and sceneries wafted through. Not at all a dislocated body, since there has never been anything but pieces of the body and there will never be a body, this wandering collection being the very affirmation of the non-body. The plural, the collection of singularities, are precisely what power, kapital, the law of value, personal identity, the ID card, responsibility, the family and the hospital are bent on repressing.

Thus, *drift*: in honor of the damned. The Odyssey displaced— not at all Ulysses' polymorphy collected and gathered, totalized in a return home, to the self, which will be the model of Hegelian dialectics and of bourgeois socialist thought and praxis in their entirety. Rather the intense stationary drift wherein the fragments clash in Joyce's *Ulysses*.

If there is a drift as regards the position of the author and the consistency of these texts, then there must also be a drift with respect to efficiency both as an idea and as a fact. There is no revolutionary efficiency, for efficiency being a concept and a practice of power, is counter-revolutionary in its very principle; there is a perception and a production of words, practices, forms, which may be revolutionary but cannot be guaranteed to be sensitive enough to drift with the great currents, the great *Triebe*, the major flows which are to displace all the visible set-ups and change the very notion of operativeness.

Which obviously implies, among other things, that no one, no subject, no group or party can legitimately take the credit for this oceanic-sismo-graphic sensitivity and that an organization can come to the point of turning such receptivity into a transforming action, a forging, grafting, "creating" action, only through an overturning which is the (open) secret of political alienation, and already includes all of power's paranoia.

It is undoubtedly useless to fight for the consistency of a political, philosophical discourse and practice, by arguing against the inconsistency of the adversary's political, philosophical discourse. Useless because, indirectly, such a battle is still a battle for reason, for unity, for the unification of diversities, a quibbling battle which no one can win for the winner is already and has always been reason. And we don't want to destroy kapital because it isn't rational, but because it is. Reason and power are one and the same thing. You may disguise the one with dialectics or prospectiveness, but you will still have the other in all its crudeness: jails, taboos, public weal, selection, genocide.

The drift must go beyond the anchorage where this book arbitrarily interrupts it. If reason, which has been handed over to the air-conditioned totalitarianism of the very disputatious end of this century, is not to be relied upon, then its great tool, its very main-spring, its provision of infinite progress, its fertile negativity, its pains and toiling—i.e. critique—shouldn't be given credit either. Let it be said very clearly: it is untrue that a political, philosophical, artistic position is relinquished through *sublation*; it is untrue that the experiencing of a position entails the complete development of its content, its exhaustion, and thus its transcrescence into another position which preserves-suppresses it, it is untrue that, in experience and discourse, the occupation of a position necessarily leads to its critique and impels you to adopt a new position which will negatively include the former one and sublate it. This description of the dialectic of Spirit by Hegel, is also that of the capitalist's getting richer and richer by Adam Smith, it is the good student's vision of life, it is in addition the thick string on which the political jumping-jacks hang their promises of happiness and with which they strangle us. There is a forgotten Freud in such an outlook: the one who dared write that the libido never relinquishes an investment for a better one, that there are rather simultaneous investments in one region of the body (of the mental apparatus, in Freud's terms) and in another, that they are *uncothinkable*, yet *compossible*, that they ignore each other but are both operative, that their efficacy is not that of different levels (e.g. semiological or epistemological levels) distinguished for the sake of analysis, that the same energy is at work in both instances, at the same level, deposited in the same place at the same time, but produces different products: e.g. jealousy centered on penis envy, anal masochism, clitoral sadism, three co-present effects of the libido's wanderings on the bodies of the women analyzed in "A Child is Being Beaten," according to Freud. What is forgotten in dialectic is that one forgets and that forgetting implies the preservation of everything, memory being but a selection.

Critique as well is a selective activity: such and such an experience, a declaration, a work of art, a political initiative, a libidinal position is exhibited in its *deficiencies*, *negated* thus, considered to be one from the point of view of its limit and not of its affirmativity, challenged to equal the object of the critic's desire, i.e. infinity, universality, necessity; it will be accepted or rejected, or rather both at the same time in every case, accepted because the critic needs an object to complain about (as the teacher needs pupils and the union workers), rejected because no object attains the required level. Selection is an infinite task, as when you enter a foreign city and follow the arrows indicating the *Zentrum*, the *centro citta*, until you lose them, the absence of indication indicating that you are at the center and rather that there is no center. Likewise, the functionary's critical-selective life follows the arrows, but when he reaches the summit he has made it and yet hasn't, because the desire for power knows no summit. Negating. This activity is deeply rational, deeply consistent with the system. Deeply reformist: the critic remains in the sphere of the criticized, he belongs to it, he goes beyond one term of the position but doesn't alter the position of terms. And deeply hierarchical: where does his power over the criticized come from? he *knows* better? he is the teacher, the educator? he is therefore universality, the University, the State, the City, bending over childhood, nature, singularity, shadiness, to reclaim them? The confessor and God helping the sinner save his soul? This benign reformism is wholly compatible with the preservation of the authoritarian relationship. Multiplying the overturns and reversals leads nowhere. The transforming activity is underhandedly privileged in all this repair shop machinery, which is the reason why the ultra-leftist revolutionary groups and micro-groups have failed: they had to display their maleness, their brawn, they had to keep the initiative. But the same idea of efficiency drives the bosses—high-level bureaucrats, business executives, decision-makers and officers. Do not say that unlike them, *we* know the desire of the "masses" (the criticized object): no one knows it, for desire baffles knowledge and power. He who pretends to know it is indeed the educator, the priest, the prince. Nothing will have changed, therefore, if while claiming to serve the desire of the masses you act according to your alleged knowledge and assume their *direction*. Where do you criticize from? Don't you see that criticizing is still knowing, knowing better? That the critical relation still falls within the sphere of knowledge, of "realization" and thus of the assumption of power? Critique must be drifted out of. Better still: *Drifting is in itself the end of all critique.*

The desire underlying and informing institutions composes set-ups which are energetic investments in the body, in language, in the earth and the city, in the difference of sexes and ages, etc. Kapitalism is one of these set-ups. There is in it nothing, no dialectic, which will lead to its sublation in socialism: Everyone knows that socialism is identical with kapitalism. Any critique, far from transcending the latter, reinforces it. What destroys it is the drift of desire, the withdrawal of cathexis, not at all where the economists look for it (the kapitalists' reluctance to invest), but the libidinal relinquishment of the system of kapital and of all its poles, is the fact that for millions of young people (irrespective of their social origin), desire no longer invests the kapitalist set-up; is that they no longer consider themselves or behave as a labor-power to be valorized with a view to exchanges, i.e. consumption, is that they locate what kapital persists in naming work, modern life, consumption, nation, family, State, ownership, profession, education, all "values" that they perceive as so many parodies of the one and only value, the exchange-value. *That* is a drift, affecting all civilizations on a worldwide scale.

No sublation whatsoever in this process: in a way, one is only witnessing the culmination of kapital, which is by no means progress, education, peace, prosperity, humanism, but simply a circulation of energy regulated by the law of ownership and the principle of the extension of its circuits. What the new generation accomplishes is the skepticism of kapital, its nihilism: there are no things, no persons, no borders, no knowledges, no beliefs, no reasons to live/die. But this nihilism is simultaneously the strongest affirmation: it contains the potential liberation of drives from the law of value, from the whole system geared to the safekeeping of properties and the preservation of the terms of exchange, and thus to the upholding of exchange itself as an "ironclad necessity." The religion of necessity does indeed nourish the gloomy and haughty thoughts of high-level bureaucrats all over the world, but it also feeds the "scientific" spirit; its compulsive rituals can be detected in the works of Freud, Spinoza, Marx and perhaps even Nietzsche's: it is what remains to be destroyed. A successful attack on the belief in necessity would inevitably lead to the destruction of kapital's very main-spring: the alleged necessity for an equal value of the terms of exchange. In its practice, the young generation occasionally anticipates this destruction, acts and thinks without consideration for equivalence, takes as its sole guide, instead of a potential return, affective intensity, the possibility of decoupling libidinal force. This is affirmative rather than critical and can be done from without all critiques, by way of a silence (in Cage's acceptation of the word), which evades and infiltrates discourse.

Another libidinal set-up which is still nebulous, difficult to discern, emerges thus in a non-dialectic, non-critical, incompossible relation with that of kapital. There is no more necessity for it to stem from kapital than there was for the rural-corporative and religious society of the Middle Ages to generate the mercantile and rationalist society of the Renaissance and the age of Classicism. And it will not necessarily overcome kapitalism. The appearance of this set-up on the social body must be understood in the same way as the cathecting of the erotic body by the libido: incompatible, random, simultaneous, discontinuous processes.

The word aesthetic has an insulting connotation in Marxist-French, which shows the links in this language with that of the bourgeoisie: contempt for art as a form of entertainment, for the artist as a buffoon, for aesthetic problems as false problems screening the real ones—all of these formal concerns being considered as superstructural irrealities. And feeding this contempt, an active repression of affective intensities on pretext that Rothko's painting, Cage's music, Baruchello's films serve no purpose, that they are not efficient, that they belong to elitism and can only maintain the cultural domination of the bourgeoisie.

Something is always happening in the arts—now the theater, now painting, or music, or the cinema (the latter being more directly placed on the orbit of kapital, however)—which incandesces the embers glowing in the depths of society. It is depressive and nihilistic to consider the region of unreality where the forms flare up as a mere deportation camp or as a cozy shelter for irresponsible elements, socially neutralized, hence politically null; the opposite is to be understood, namely that "artists" want society as a whole to reach this unreality, want the repression and suppression of libidinal intensities by the so-called seriousness, which is only the torpescence of kapitalist paranoia, to be lifted everywhere, and show how to do it by working and removing the most elementary obstacles, those opposing to desire the *No* of the alleged reality, the perception of times, spaces, colors, volumes.

They show parts of bodies restituted to their wandering, to their libidinal intensity, and fragments of objects, surfaces, durations, depths, chromatic and tonal sequences, with which something like an orgasmic death can happen. They think nothing is more serious. They deem the pseudo-seriousness of authorities and Kapital, their "reality" delivered by dint of unfounded fears, frightful and miserable. They distrust politicians, their pretention to universality inherited from philosophers, and to directorship bequeathed by pedagogues. "Aesthetics" has been for the politicist I was (and still am?), not at all an alibi, a comfortable retreat, but the fault and fracture giving access to the subsoil of the political scene, the great vault of a cave on which the overturned or reversed recesses of this scene could be explored, a pathway allowing me to skirt or divert it. For the operations concealed in the production of ideologies can be induced from those of desire exhibited in the production of "works" of art. Hence the equation: aesthetics = workshop for the forging of the most discriminative critical concepts.

But this equation, which belongs to Adorno (whose works I had not read when the essays collected here were written) still doesn't drift enough. Art, in the critique factory, is not a workshop for the making of tools. The most modern trends—American abstracts, pop and hyper-realism in painting and sculpture, poor and concrete musics (Cage's above all), free choreographies (Cunningham's), intensity theaters (if they exist)—place critical thought and negative dialectics before a considerable challenge: the works they produce are affirmative, not critical. They aver a new position of desire, the traces of which have just been referred to. The philosopher and the politicist (whose thinking you are about to consider) would have been content, after Adorno, with using the arts as formal reversal matrices; they are nonetheless required to have an eye and an ear, a mouth and a hand for the new position, which is the end of all critique. They might find this difficult: what if it were their own end as well?

Translated by Roger McKeon

On Theory: An Interview

Brigitte Devismes——*What does theoretical research mean to you today?*

J.-F. Lyotard—your question really puzzles me, for the word "theoretical" covers an almost limitless number of fields. The answer might require delimiting the field I am currently exploring; at any rate, what I am interested in, even if this isn't the correct approach, is the fact that, politically, we have no theory, although important segments of a theory could take their inspiration from what is happening in the "arts." Maybe this is what I could elaborate on. There are three things I would like to say, in fact. The first one concerns political theory, and I choose this "example" because it seems to me that the function of theory is not only to understand, but also to criticize, i.e. to call in question and *overturn* a reality, social relationships, the relationships of men with things and other men, which are clearly intolerable. And as far as I am concerned, *that* is the dimension of politics. It isn't only the assumption of power, it must consist in the overturning of a mystified or alienated reality. Marxism, which was all the same an effective theory, has obviously been useful in this regard, but in the situation we know today, and have known for at least a decade, in fact, traditional Marxism isn't wholly satisfactory from a theoretical point of view.

——*Hasn't Althusser efficiently updated Marxism?*

——Althusser's contribution is important, indeed, but I am not sure he is on the right track, although different aspects of his work are undoubtedly relevant. He has attempted to extract from Marxism a theory that would be in a properly theoretical relation with the field of social experience. A relation which would no longer be dialectical, within which the order of experience and that of discourse would be entirely separated. In which regard I believe he is right, for it is true that a theory is not in a dialectical relation with the field it applies to. And anything having to do with a process, a genesis, a passage from the objective to the subjective, in the Hegelian sense, must in effect be rejected as a religiouslike mystification, a reconciliation phantasy. This, I don't intend to explain, but it is now obvious to me that what is left of Hegelian dialectics in the traditional Marxist approach makes it into something similar to a religion. Where Althusser sould not be followed, however, where something obviouly breaks down, is where he suddenly stops and reserves the political dimension for the Party—the so-called "Communist" party. What incites him to do so, in fact, is that he considers this dimension as belonging to an ideological order, in which the problem raised is not that of truth, but of efficiency. I believe something is false in this global configuration of the relation between theory and practice as elaborated by Althusser. False because the critical dimension of theory has disappeared. What is at stake is not only a conceptual type of critique, it is a *practical* one.

——*And what you tax him with, if I am not mistaken, is failing to conceptualize the alienation within which he is currently working, and to criticize it.*

——Exactly. When he eliminates alienation as a concept that doesn't belong in the system, he is right, but when he says that there is no room for alienation in Marxist theory, he is wrong. As such, the concept obviously doesn't belong to the system which allows us to understand what capitalism is. There is no room for alienation at that level, it is not a concept relating to the order of the reproduction of capital, but a fact which belongs to the realm of social experience, what Marx used to name "representations and perceptions," and it is extremely important, precisely because, in this realm, it points to the possibility of a theory, of a *true* universality. One must understand that alienation is the experiencing of a false, abstract universality. It consists, for example, in the fact that anything can be exchanged for anything else, through the mediation of money. Or the fact that the relation between the worker and his work is an indifferent relation, in Marx's words. Any worker can do any work, permutations change nothing, which is what reveals alienation. At the experiential level, alineation can be characterized as the experiencing of an abstract universality, the universal being cut off from concrete situations. Money, for example, is an abstract universal, i.e. it can be exchanged for any object and in a proportion entirely independent from the use of the objects for which it is exchanged. Likewise, the relation of the salaried worker with what he does is an abstract universal relation: he mediatizes the materials and the machinery, but this relation is external to him, it is a false mediation; in fact, labor-power is but a transitory incarnation of capital, which is why the encounter of the worker and his work becomes a random one. I consider it extremely important that these phenomena—which are explicitly described in Marx's works—be taken into consideration, for without them, the possibility of a theory would never arise, whereas in precapitalist societies the abstract universality I just mentioned didn't exist; when it began to appear in the mercantile sector, its scope was limited to very small segments of society and, more importantly still, it didn't affect the worker himself, who wasn't salaried. In today's capitalist society, this abstraction tends to spread to *all* activities.

——*How do you link alienation and this possibility of theorizing? I might even ask how you conciliate them.*

The question is not that of a conciliation. Let us say that if there aren't in the realm of social experience, on the very level at which the theorist finds himself, if there aren't in the brain which is attempting to conceptualize this experience, inasmuch as this brain belongs to experience—i.e. in the most immediate field, in the phenomenal field where social relationships are located—if there aren't indices which refer to the possibility of a systematic understanding of things, indices that function negatively in sum, which are like holes in this experience, holes through which one is going to see, or attempt to see, at least, what organizes this lacunary experience which is that of capitalist society with its alienation . . . then there is no possibility of a theory. I don't say that the *theory* becomes *necessary*. If the actual conditions of experience didn't already contain—in a negative way—the index of a universality, there is no reason why this universality could be constructed as a system. Which is why Marxism is not possible before capitalism, as Marx himself has shown it in the 1857 introduction to *A Contribution to the Critique of Political Economy* that Althusser likes to quote so much, but in my opinion misinterprets.

——*How do you define this theory made possible by universality?*

——I give it the strictly formal meaning any modern logician would, and understand it as the consitution of a set of terms and of the operative relations and laws which will allow the elements of this set to enter into different combinations. It is undeniable that, in this sense, Marx did construct the theory of capitalism by defining the general formula for capital, by elaborating, for example, the concept of the organic composition and the transformational law of this composition. Such is the definition of a theory that I should like to adopt here. But I also want to stress that the problems currently encountered in all developed countries pertain to an appendix of this theory which Marx never really theorized, something he always assumed, rather, and that might precisely be a residue of Hegelian dialectics, namely that starting from this system within which a labor-power functions as one of the *moments* in the realization of capital, one tends to take an awakening of the proletariat for granted. Perhaps I am expressing myself abstractly. . . To put it otherwise, Marx, in my opinion, offers both a theory and a hypothesis concerning class struggle; now, the latter cannot be deduced from the former—it has nothing to do with the theoretical field: it belongs to social experience. It is true that social experience involves class struggle, conflicts between employers and workers and, in a broader perspective, between managers and realizers, but it cannot legitimately be inferred from the laws established in the theoretical order that this struggle leads to socialism. Class struggles belong to the phenomenological order.

——*The problem now, is to dissociate the two orders, to show where theory and practice stand, because talking about theoretical practice isn't sufficient, neither is saying that theory is impossible in the absence of a practice and vice versa . . .*

——Indeed, this is what has started to emerge in Althusser's works, i.e. the recognition that there is a theoretical order, which is that of the general formula for capital, of the origin of surplus-value and of the fate of capitalism on the one hand, and the practice of class struggle on the other, the existence of which cannot be denied in the order of what Marx called "perceptions and representations," the acknowledgement, moreover, that the two orders are no longer connected. The reasons we had to believe, let us say that the revolutionaries had to believe, fifty years ago, in the proletariat as the privileged locus of crises and social critique, well, these reasons have lost their cogency. One cannot say that the proletariat is this locus in any of the developed countries; it just isn't true.

——*Then, where is this locus? Could it be that you situate it in the University?*

——I don't know if there is a locus. One cannot say that there is a privileged spot where society becomes aware of itself, or criticizes itself, without going back to Hegel. This would mean that the order of theory, e.g. the law of the organic composition of capital, is in a continuous relation with the order of social experience, the phenomenological order, and that it promotes the progress of awareness and critique in the latter. I don't believe in this continuity. . . It seems to me that the relation between the order of theory and that of class struggle has nothing to do with what can be said about it from within a Hegelian perspective. It can only be defined negatively. The only thing we can say is that, as it develops, the capitalist system invests activities which had formerly been unaffected by it, e.g. teaching and studying; alienation thus makes its appearance and takes over in such sectors. This is also true as far as "art" goes. . . What I mean is that the experiencing of alienation extends way beyond the proletariat and that it is therefore perfectly understandable that fractions of society which cannot be said to be exploited in the strict sense of the term—the student body being one of these—seriously challenge society. All that can be said, and this is to state it negatively, is this: As long as the victims of true exploitation—i.e. labor-power as the source of surplus-value—don't refuse to keep on being merchandises in the system, the system can last on. . . as long, at any rate, as its *intrinsic* contradictions allow it to hold out. And at least one of these contradictions exists, but it does not *necessarily lead to a revolution.* This is what should be said; this is how the problem is now posed.

——*What is this intrinsic contradiction?*

——Marx puts it very clearly. . . There is actually only one, being that the system appraises all values in terms of working time and that it tends, through its own dynamic, to reduce working time to a minimum. The pursuit of profit aims at this reduction. Nonetheless, the whole accountancy of value is based on working time. One of the effects is that the system cannot give everyone work and that it tends to give out less and less.

——*Isn't surplus-value itself another contradiction in the system?*

——This raises another problem. If surplus-value can be reinvested, the system grows; its growth means that goods, activities, objects which were not capitalistically invested are going to be. That is the general process. The question is to know whether a time will come when surplus-value can no longer be reinvested. Of course, there are overcapitalization crises, but experience has shown that, until now, different safety-valves— e.g. waging wars, sending things to the moon—have always been found. There is one problem, however, for which there is no safety-valve, namely that merchandise can be produced today with ten times, a hundred times, in some cases even a thousand times less labor-power than a hundred years ago, and this is a very serious problem.

——Yes, but more and more things are being produced . . .

——That are not given away. . . So, if folks have no work, they won't be able to buy them. That is what is happening in the Third World as is only too obvious. In this sense, it is true that Third World populations are today's industrial reserve. At the risk of being considered incoherent, I will now deal with my second point: what the practice of "art" or the crisis in the "arts" can teach us.

——You mentioned earlier that the arts were now invested by the system and my intention was precisely to ask you what this entails for the artist.

——I would prefer not to answer your question because I am not competent in this regard. I believe that those we call "artists" are the first ones to realize the fact and they know more about it than I do. . . I can describe the fantastic way in which teaching has been invested by the system over the last fifteen years; but as far as the so-called artistic activity goes, I believe others would be in a better position to elaborate than I am. What I did mean to dwell on is the tradition according to which political critique and "art" criticism are kept completely separate. Politicists consider artists as jesters, that is they share the bourgeois point of view on the artist. And artists ignore politicists in general. Now, what strikes me is that we are witnessing both an enormous crisis in the "arts", on account of which the word "art" has practically been relinquished and, in my view, just as serious a political crisis. (The re-constitution of micro-groups of a traditional type does not change this crisis at all, it only masks and manifests it.) It seems to me that it is precisely on account of the short or long term relinquishment, of the necessary relinquishment of Marxist *dialectics* considered as a religiouslike ideology, that practices which are much more closely related to the activity of the "artist" than they are to political activities in the traditional sense began to develop as soon as May 1968 in France and have been adopted by movements such as the German SDS. I believe that what is important in this "artistic" practice—I put the word in quotation marks because I don't think art can be all that easily defined and because I do think this artistic function is currently becoming impossible—what is important is that the impossibility of this function proceeds from the same reasons as those on account of which a certain political ideology can no longer be pursued.

——*When would you say this crisis dates from?*

——I would say it started at the end of the 19th century, when, between 1880 and 1920, a whole series of things which signified a complete mutation of the "specialist's" relation to form began to appear. The function of the artist, from then on, is no longer to produce *good* forms, new good forms, but on the contrary to *deconstruct* them systematically and to accelerate their obsolescence. And this indefinitely, by attacking these good forms on all levels. As far as the musical code is concerned, for example, the old scale is dropped and dodecaphony invented; or the note as the musician's traditional material is forgotten and music is made with noises. The same can be done with the medium in plastic arts, e.g. Heizer digging hole in Nevada.

——Buren criticizes this aspect of the process. He points out that doing things in the desert is no solution and the problem is to bring them to the city, where the best neon production risks being outshined by the electric sign on the corner drugstore. . .

——Yes, I believe he is completely right. But it is interesting all the same, from an experimental point of view, because an attempt is made to deconstruct the traditional space of sculpture and to invert it; what Heizer produces is a sunk carving on the earth itself. Maybe this is why he has to work in the countryside... because he starts from this primary hypothesis. So, in spite of the fact that the social effect is nil, it is an interesting attempt, one example of a deconstruction among thousands of others, Surrealism having been a mere episode from this point of view, nothing more. . . Only *from this point of view though*, I insist.

——What is positive is thus deconstruction?

——I don't know whether it is positive; I would rather call it negative, but it is what I deem important. You cannot consider what has been happening in painting, music or sculpture for almost a century without having the feeling that the function of art has overturned. Art no longer plays the role it used to, for it once had a religious function, it created good forms, some sort of a myth, of a ritual, of a rhythm, a medium other than language through which the members of a society would communicate by participating in a same music, in a common substratum of meaning. . . And this generally went on in churches. Daily life was the realm of discourse, but the sacred was that of form, i.e. that of art. This has now become impossible. Why? Because we are in a system that doesn't give a rap about sacredness.

——*It has liquidated the sacred, hasn't it?*

——Yes, it has absolutely liquidated all of this because it is only interested in what can be sold. Thus the artist himself tends to become part of the labor-power, etc. But what I believe to be extremely important is not so much the way the artist has reacted to his social position, but the manner in which he has reacted to the situation capitalism has created as far as his activity goes: instead of continuing to produce unifying, reconciling forms, his activity has become a deconstructing one which is necessarily critical. And I would be tempted to say, in spite of my interest in politics, that the best, the most radical critical activity bears on the formal, the most directly plastic aspect of painting, photography or the film, and not so much on the *signified*, be it social or anything else, of the object it is concerned with. More specifically, I would say that Mallarmé's work—in *Le Coup de dés*, for example—on the very space of the printed sheet, is an extremely important critical work insofar as it shows that the typographical space itself is one conquered on a plastic space, which resists it, which is suppressed by the space of discourse. And precisely in *Le Coup de dés*, this plastic space is suggested, restituted as the other of the discursive and textual space. They will surely say that this has no political impact whatsoever. . . but I am not sure they won't be wrong.

——*What do these deconstructions contribute? Can they be politically annexed? Furthermore, aren't the terms "revolutionary art" self-contradictory?*

——Indeed they are, and completely irrelevant. Every time an attempt at revolutionary art was made it turned out to be a catastrophe, which is quite understandable, since it meant that art yielded to the requirements of a political *discourse* and, consequently, lost all freedom to deconstruct. Which was the drama in Breton's relation with the Communist party, which could just as well be the drama—or the buffoonery—in the relation of any of today's artists with more than one micro-group.

——*But is deconstruction an action?*

——Yes, you've just raised the right question: does politics ultimately consist in producing organizations which could replace those currently in power, after having destroyed them on the one hand, and, on the other, is what the artistic deconstruction produces an action? The two questions are linked. I believe it is absolutely obvious today, and has been for quite some time that, for one thing, the reconstitution of traditional political organizations, even if they present themselves as ultra-leftist organizations is bound to fail, for these settle precisely into the order of the social surface, they are "recovered," they perpetuate the type of activity the system has instituted as political, they are necessarily alienated, ineffective. The other thing is that all the deconstructions which could appear as aesthetic formalism, "avant-garde" research, etc., actually make up the only type of activity that is effective, this because it is functionally—the word is very bad, *ontologically* would be better and more straightforward—located outside the system; and, by definition, its function is to deconstruct everything that belongs to order, to show that all this "order" conceals something else, that it represses.

——*To show that this order is based on no justifiable authority?*

——Yes. And this deconstructing activity is a truly radical critical activity for it does not deal with the *signifieds* of things, but with their plastic organization, their signifying organization. It shows that the problem is not so much that of knowing what a given discourse says, but rather how it is disposed. It shows that it is active on account of its very disposition, its configuration, and that the deconstruction of its disposition is going to reveal all of its mystifying content.

———*Should one make a distinction between the level on which art theoreticians see what this critique consists in, and that on which the artist works? In other words, does critique really proceed from within the arts?*

———Perhaps a distinction should be made. . . but I believe that it is more and more difficult to be an "artist" today, without adopting a critical position. We no longer live in a time where artists belonged to a studio, to a school, where the function of the forms to be produced was not to cause events, as it is today, but on the contrary to play an integrative role. In painting or "literature," for example, it is absolutely impossible to produce anything without reflecting on its critical function—i.e. considering carefully what is to be dealt with, for example, in what type of space the written or pictural signs are going to be produced. There is more and more anti-art in this sense. I imagine there will always be a difference between artists and theorists, but that is rather a good thing, for theorists have everything to learn from the artists, even if the latter won't do what the former expect. . .; so much the better in fact, for theorists need to be practically critized by works that disturb them.

———*Do the actions of the Movement of March 22[1] inspire the parallel you draw between deconstruction on the artistic level and political critique?*

———Yes, I am indeed thinking of a type of action which closely resembles what they used to call "examplary action" at that time, which coincides with it in fact. The Movement had this idea, which wasn't an idea. . . , yes, maybe it was after all. . . , which was surprising in itself, and according to which this deconstructing activity should be transferred into the places and institutions of everyday social practice. And it was then recognized that this had an extraordinarily *revolutionary* function, in the right sense of the term, I believe. The question was no longer of singing the praises of an organization, but of starting to criticize the system *here and now*, not at all in the signified of its discourse, but in the actual deconstruction of its time and space.

——*Wasn't this a model for the hook-up between theory and practice towards which political action should tend?*

——Precisely, for it seems to me that what was taking place was a fulgurant junction, a flash of lightning between theory and practice—the most immediate practice and the theory perhaps the most elaborated that we have known in the last forty years. And I believe that in so doing, the Movement was in some respects answering the problems of art. For the museum is also an institution, and as long as art remains within it, it is stuck. It must come out of the museum and suppress itself as art and as a leisurely activity directed to people who are exhausted by alienation. And its coming out would be a transgression. If you start building mobiles and variable volumes, digging trenches or covering advertising posters with color in the middle of town, you are patently transgressing the order of the institution and exposing its repressive character. You are showing that the poster which was benignantly inviting us to phantasize was but a pseudo-phantasy regulated by the system, and that whoever wants to depart from the rule is rejected.

——*Even those who understand what this type of action aims at often object that "you offer nothing to replace what you are destroying. . ." What can you answer them? The argument is important because it blocks people. . .*

——No, in my opinion the problem is unimportant and

irrelevant: we are *called on to* produce the theses of a new school, and that is out of the question. That's finished, it is no longer possible. I believe demystification is an endless task. This is where the concept of a "permanent revolution" can be given its true dimension.

——*Thus the society to be hoped for is that in which one is perpetually carrying out a demystifying action and this demystification should not be based on the illusory assumption that a perfect society can be established where it would no longer be necessary?*

——Absolutely. Such a state does not exist. Even if we managed to put an end to certain forms of exploitation and oppression, the deconstruction of what is written, taken for granted, what is connotated—habits, institutions, non subverted phantasies—would be an interminable task. What was once part of the avant-garde always becomes part of the rear-guard and, as such, loses its disruptive power. That, is the strength of the capitalist system, its capacity for recovering anything and everything. In this sense, the "artists" are pushed forward, they are literally chased out of the very deconstructed forms they produce, they are compelled to keep on finding something else. I believe their research knows no other drive.

——*Works of art seduce the eye, we like them, etc. Why is it that they please us?*

——I would be tempted to say that what pleases us now is what disconcerts us, and in this sense we are really in Freud's "death drive." What we are interested in is the dimension of otherness, alteration. There is a constant displacement and this displacement as such is what we are interested in, the fact that we are disconcerted, put out of time, caught on the wrong foot... Yes, the absence of a locus. Pontalis spoke of a Freudian utopia in the strong sense of the word. He meant that there was a non-locus. Well, what pleases us disconcerts us because it points to a non-locus.

Edited and translated by Roger McKeon

Note

1. The Movement began on March 22, 1968, at the University of Nanterre, near Paris; led by Daniel Cohn-Bendit (Danny le Rouge), an anarchistic sociology student, it was instrumental in bringing about the May '68 "revolution" in France.

Jewish Oedipus

I

There is, in Freud's work, a language of knowledge and there is a truth-work. They keep one another company. The first is sustained by Helmholtz; it manifests itself in the *Project for a Scientific Psychology* (1895), in the unflagging elaboration of the topographies. It aims at constructing itself in theory, on a plane that would be absent from that it speaks of. Neither the system's being consistantly disordered, as the beginning of *Instincts and their Vicissitudes* (1915) states, nor the theory's endless closing up, prevent our having to do with a linguistic space that is closed in principle. Freud's genius is to treat these disorders not as obstacles, but as revelations.

It is within the language of cognition itself that desire displaces, condenses, suppresses, subverts regular relations, leaves traces. The trace of desire is not a scripture, but a transgression of writing, just as the operations by which desire takes hold of the *Traumgedanke* ("dreamthoughts")[1] and converts it into the oneiric mise-en-scène deconstruct the clear residues of diurnal discourse and perception. Truth *doesn't speak, stricto sensu*; it works. Cognition speaks, it belongs to distance, to the rupture with things that discourse requires. It produces a theory within the space of possibility, freed from things, and seeks afterwards to find in things what can serve as a referential model for its discourse, as a field of interpretation. Truth is not what operates this secondary disjunction. It leaves its traces on discourse, the fulguration of a slip, a silence, a forbidden metaphor, a portmanteau word, a non-sense, a cry; but its effects come from *elsewhere*, signaling their strangeness in that they do violence to the order (of regulated language) in which they inscribe themselves. Spoken language, be it that of cognition, serves here to mirror these truth effects. André Green says this very well of literary works:

> In the long sequence of signifiers whose chain constitutes the work, the unconscious signified rises up between two signifiers from the absence where it keeps itself and compels the difference between the "natural" form of discourse and its literary form. Not in order to express therein what is to be said, but to show, by veiling it, what is to be hidden.[2]

One can, one must draw from the other stage's mode of presence in discourse a riposte to writing's integrism; which is just what André Gree does (*Ibid.*, "Prologue").

The rule of free association and that of suspended attention, Jean Laplanche recalled recently,[3] operate as a *speculum* on the language of signification, which is that of communication and knowledge, with its principles of pertinence and economy; they maintain language open to what, coming from elsewhere, leaves its mark upon it; they keep it from closing up by unpriming and repressing the figures of truth. The work of deconstruction comes to meet the other work, that of the unconscious, by dismantling the bastion of signification. The anti-logic of meaning will find, in this area stretched out between the tedious words forever dwelling on reasons, the screen on which to trace its figures; not the figure itself, lost like Eurydice, but the figure's lateral, peripheral inscriptions, like the few lines Cézanne traces with watercolor in 1905, that seem to have come from the other side of the white sheet of paper, with which the eye is left to compare and identify the figure whose shatters they are, Mont Sainte-Victoire. Planted before the mountain for hours on end, what does Cézanne do? He freely associates, he maintains an evenly suspended, indiscriminating attention to what thing-bound and gestaltist perception make us not see. He deconstructs an order, a scripture; he wants to see the bad, the wrong form, to see what active, adaptive focalization represses at the periphery of the field: the anamorphoses, the curves, the obliques, the laterals.

Art is the locus of this double reversal where the space of

disseizure, that all phantasy encloses and upon which it is reclosed as on the lack of signifier from which it proceeds, returns to offer itself from the outside to that profound figure which may thus inscribe its traces upon it. Something like this: the interior space, that which refuses all reception, which grips the primitive figure, escapes from it, turns around, returns to invest it and offers a stage for its operations. The work of art is a symptom inasmuch as it *is* a set of traces referable in principle to a primal phantasy; it differs from one in that it *bears* these traces; exhibits them. Trace bearing trace, a representation which is itself representative. This implies that desire is desired, not in order to say it, to theorize it, but in order to see it. And one must not even affirm: so that others may see it, in order to make a work out of it; because it is not true that painting and literature progress in the survey of these figures on account of "authors," on account of those who want to "make a work of art"; they, on the contrary, have never gained but by the imprudence of those who are ready to give all past or promised works for a glimpse, be it fleeting, of the faceless figure.

Theatre is the dream in that it fascinates and amounts to an hallucination giving rise to identification; and it is not the dream, it is the dream redoubled, the scene of the dream set on *its* own stage, the figural space of phantasy installed in its figural space of representation. This does not at all mean that phantasy, that the unconscious process in general, is mastered in dramatic creation. The unconscious process is not controllable. The theatre, on the contrary, shows that it is our master; it shows us disseized, it manifests cognition's failure to recognize, the delusion of whoever inquires in order to know, of Oedipus. And it *shows* this, that is to say it disseizes us in our turn, effectively, we spectators, since it is a scene, a fascinating figure, at the same time as it is true. Indissociable truth and disseizure. As André Green puts it:

> Truth, says Freud at the end of his work, is only attained by its deformations, deformations which are not the doing of some falsifier, but which are a necessity for all men who want to avoid the displeasure bound

with the revelation of the inadmissible. This constraint is the *deformative constraint*. Whence the lack of recognition when the truth arises. (*Ibid.*, p. 282).

And more clearly still:

> What can be said of the Oedipus knot is not that it is an inaccessible signified, but a signified that offers itself only in its absence. This absence is not an inexistence, nor an absconding from all attempts at a seizure... The dream, the symptom, inhabited by *unconscious representation*, speak this absence. An absence that would not be the reflection of death, but death in life itself, in the replication of lack, insofar as it traces and shifts it. The theatre takes up the wager of invoking this absence in the most scandalous manner, since nowhere does language hold forth the discourse of presence with more ostentation. . . In the theatre absence must be sought lurking in the redoubling of speech spoken again. (*Ibid.*, p. 286-287).

II

Jean Starobinski has collected, in his preface to Jones' *Hamlet and Oedipus*,[4] all the passages concerning Oedipus in Freud's work and correspondence and he has ascertained that references to Hamlet are accompanied by references to Oedipus from the beginning, starting with a letter to Fliess dated 1897. He is thus led to recognize in these tragic figures a mediating function "between Freud's past and Freud's patient" (p. xxxxvi), a mediation that supports the following system of analogies: Me is like Oedipus; Oedipus was us; Hamlet is Oedipus again; Hamlet is the neurotic (pp. xxxv ff).

This group of transformations is what articulates the figures in which Freud's desire to see/know is fulfilled. In detecting such a group, I believe that Jean Starobinski not only brings us admirably close to what *truth-work* may be, but that he also informs us of the capital fact that this work operates through the mediation of the tragic scene, and, finally, that he sets us off on an important track: Hamlet's unaccomplishment of the paternal word as modernity's difference from the Greek world.

The first of these operations of truth is a comparison, the other three metaphors. They all signify a transport of identity under different proper names. These names appear as masks or face values: they stand for something else. They are figures which can be faced, announcing another, faceless, figure. These figures are ordered in depth according to a tree: from that of Oedipus, placed at the greatest depth, directly proceeds the displacement of *me to us*, and from this group to Hamlet; that of Hamlet commands a second generation, a second bearing of displacement, that which will permit the identification of the group me-us in the neurotic, and make psychoanalytic practice possible.

By what right these displacements and this hierarchy of figures? Where has Freud ever set forth their premises? What theory grounds them, what theory do they ground? Irrelevant questions. Something, a name, a destiny, can stand for something else without the rules of substitution or transformation ever being announced. We are at the antipodes of science; it is easy for us, after Freud as it happens, to recognize in these unexpected displacements operations of the unconscious process; they take place in non-recognition, in another place. But is this precisely not the error, the delusion that such displacements give rise to, they that cause one thing to be taken for another? Is it not mad to take as truth-work what is dream-work?

III

This is where the reversal on the dramatic stage intervenes and founds the "piece of daring" of which Starobinski speaks (*Ibid.* p. xxxvi). To take oneself for Oedipus would in fact be dream-work, an unconscious process of identification, if Oedipus

were a simple figure. But Oedipus is an overturned figure.
Sophocles produces Oedipus, the simple figure, which is in fact the
figure of non-recognition, he brings it into view. Putting on stage
the *text* that the prince endeavors to weave around the pestilence
that strikes Thebes in order to account for it, he manifests it as an
aberration; the errant subject comes forward as a hero, as figural
fate, with his noisy words, his unknowing knowledge. What pushes
him forward, what manifests his deviation, is the presence of the
traces of truth; presence that will say its last word through the
mouth of Tiresias. The event of the profound figure of parricidal
and incestuous desire scans the drama, leading the wandering
seeker back again and again (on seven occasions from the
encounter with the priest of the pestilence in the very beginning to
the testimony of the Herdsman, lines 1110-1185) in the direction of
this figure.

The bewilderment is manifested, in the chains of reason that
Oedipus fabricates, by the event of a trace. The text of
reason/unreason serves as the mirror on which a line coming from
elsewhere may appear. The figural space, the topological space of
transgression in which his phantasy offers him his father to kill and
his mother as wife, returns to invest the phantastic figure and to
offer the figure to us to be seen. Theatrical staging is not the
repetition of the phantastic mise-en-scène, but its double reversal,
its placing in a space that presents the same properties as that of
the unconscious. Instead of phantasy erecting the stage and
arranging the figures so as to fulfill desire, it is Sophocles—i.e. the
desire to see this phantasy—who offers the dramatic space in
which it may fulfill its non-recognition, but also its operations,
visibly. The properties of the unconscious space, that Freud has
described as we know in paragraph V of *The Unconscious* (1915),
appear on stage in the form of the *event*, an unjustified event,
violating the laws of logic and the rules of ethics. No reason for it is
given and through it is manifested the unreason of reasonability
and rationality.

Freud's identifying himself with Oedipus is not an identification; it is , as indeed Jean Starobinski says, a recognition, neither

cognition nor non-recognition, but a representation of his own phantastic figure in Sophocles' re-presentation of that of Oedipus. There is an infinite power of replication in the figure:[5] for it is itself, in its most archaic position—that which Freud called primal phantasy—already cleavage, it is at the same time unpresentable matrix and phantastic spectacle, at the same time inside and outside. With the theatre, the outside of the figure, its staging, exhibits traces of the matrix, its inside.

Truth-work consists in making the stage free for the figural event by allowing attention to float evenly on all the constituents of the errant one's discourse so that the cry or the slip or the silence coming from elsewhere may be heard. Theodore Reik said of the rule of free-floating attention that it requires of the analyst a third ear. King Oedipus has an eye too many, wrote Hölderlin. The difference between theatrical action and psychoanalytic practice does not lie in the quantity of replication, which is the same in both, but in the field of replication. In both cases, the sensory supplement is obtained by a surplus of deconstruction in the direction of the latent; but in one case it is in order to hear, in the other to see. Freud will leave Sophocles, or rather Shakespeare, when he attempts to say (the order of hearing) what tragedy shows. A return to the text, but not a return to cognition, for Freud has passed through representation's overturning, and he will not cease to make his own discourse of knowledge pass through it, reversing his text by events comparable to those that scan Oedipus' inquiry; the death drives, last event, will mark the theory the place of facelessness and of the unsignifiable, the limit of representation and of theory.

IV

But what about Hamlet? Why this position of second representation, of re-presentation of the Oedipal figure? Freud immediately noted the difference: in the letter to Fliess of October 15, 1897, that gives Starobinski his point of departure, Freud situates Hamlet as an hysteric (from the following symptoms: the expression: "Thus conscience doth make cowards of us all" (III.i.83); the hesitation in avenging the father; the denial of sexuality *vis à vis* Ophelia; a death analogous to the father's which is at the same time a punishment for his own inaction). Let us leave diagnosis aside and ask ourselves: in the order of representation, what is there in *Hamlet* that is not in *Oedipus*?

There is unaccomplishment. This can be seen as the psychological dimension of neurosis or the tragic dimension of thought. It has quite another dimension. Oedipus fulfills his fate of desire; the fate of Hamlet is the non-fulfillment of desire; this chiasma is the one that extends between what is Greek and what is Jewish, between the tragic and the ethical.

In Greek tragedy traces of the profound figure, in which we are disseized of an origin, are able to show themselves. This does not make a reconciliation [in spite of what Freud has said, for example in *Creative Writers and Day-Dreaming* (1908), or in the *Formulations on Two Principles of Mental Functioning* (1911)] but it does make re-presentation; the field is left "free" for the play of the primary process within the secondary. And to be sure the first will *toy with us*! Nevertheless this disseizure (of the spectator in tragedy) is the game to play (that makes us its play-things) for the fulguration of truth. Here discourse has not repressed the figure, it seeks to host it, it becomes desire, plays desire; this is what will always fascinate Freud, and what, he knows from the start, he will always be kept at a distance from.

In Hebraic ethics representation is forbidden, the eye closes, the ear opens in order to hear the father's word. The image figure is rejected because of its fulfillment of desire and delusion; its function of truth is denied. "Hearing," writes Rudolf Bultman, "is the way to perceive God. . . Hearing is the fact—abolishing all distance— —of knowing oneself seized, of recognizing the claim of he who speaks."[7] Thus one does not *speculate*, one does not ontologize, as Emmanuel Levinas would say. What difficulty in holding fascination at a distance!

How to be opposed to the name of God, who indeed, never shows himself, who does not speak, who spoke to be sure on Mt. Sinai, but concerning whom it was never known if He spoke for a long time, if He said all that he is credited with, if He didn't limit himself to the first sentence, to the first word, or even to the first letter of The Decalogue, which, as by chance, is the unpronounceable *alef*! What are worth the attributes and promises ascribed to a God so enigmatic? What are all the abstractions and subtleties of the Revelation worth alongside the splendid apparition of the children of the earth who wear the sun for a medallion?[8]

Yet the ethical subject knows himself seized by an Other who has spoken; he knows himself disseized of an origin, "elected" in the "irrecusable election by the Good which is, for the elected, always now and henceforth fulfilled"; elected in "a passivity more passive than all passivity: filial"; and this passivity "does not become eros, nothing suppresses in this passivity the trace of the Other in his virility in order to reduce the Other to the Same. The an-archaic bond between the subject and the Good links to an outside."[9]

The difference between the Other, the Father who has spoken, the dead voice or the voice of the dead on one side and, on the other, me the Son, Hamlet, is not a revocable difference; and if it is not, it is due to Evil. Due, says Levinas, "to the very egoism of the Self posing itself as its own origin" (p. 336). (Oh Oedipus, race of Laius, race of warriors born straight from the earth, without parents!) If this presumptive autonomy were lacking, disseizure would be unknown, passivity would be another nature, not the Good; God would be a fact. It is necessary that the son *not fulfill* the word, that no hope of reconciliation, making the Other return to the bosom of the Same, be permitted, that the son's seizure by the voice be older than his liberty, and that his liberty be the sin, the crime, of the impossible repossession.

The teaching that is the Tora cannot come to the human

person through the effect of a choice: what has to be
received in order to make free choice possible cannot
have been chosen, except *après-coup*.[10] In the
beginning was violence. Unless it were an assent other
than that which is made after scrutiny and that death
threaten an infidelity. . . Liberty as taught by the Jewish
text begins in non-liberty, which—far from being
slavery or childhood—is beyond liberty. (*Quatre
lectures*, pp. 82, 83).

There is no reconciliatory dialectic, no philosophical optimism.
"The Jews remain particularly insensitive about Jesus. . . The
Bible provides the symbols, but the Talmud does not 'fulfill'' the
Bible as the New Testament claims to fulfill and also prolong the
Old" (*Ibid.*, pp. 73, 19).

The ethical rejection affects not only ontological fulfillment,
that of Christ, but also that of cognition, the Odyssey of knowledge.
The latter is denounced as an odyssey of the self, as desire simply
to be tempted, to have been tempted, and to come out intact from
the "test":

The tempted self is still outside, it can listen to the song
of the sirens without jeopardizing the return to its
island. It can brush, can hear evil without succumbing
to it, try it without being affected by it, put it to test
without experiencing it, take risks in security (*Ibid.*, pp.
73, 74).

Such is in the eyes of the Jew, "the European certain at least of his
subject's retreat, secure in his extra-territorial subjectivity,
certain of his separation with regard to the Whole" (*Ibid.*, p. 78).

Allow me to place beside Levinas' rejection this diagnosis by
Freud:

The feeling of security with which I follow the hero
through his dangerous adventures is the same as that
with which a real hero throws himself into the water to

save a drowning man, or exposes himself to the fire of the enemy while storming a battery. It is this very feeling of being a hero which one of our best authors [Auzengruber] has so well expressed in the famous phrase, 'Nothing can happen to me!' It seems to me, however, that this significant mark of invulnerability very clearly betrays—His Majesty the Ego, the hero of all day-dreams and all novels.[11]

To this same that digests all Other, Levinas in *Quatre lectures talmudiques* opposes his reading of the *Treatise* "Chabat" (88a, 88b), which comments on *Exodus*, 19, 17, and where he finds this:

Rav Simaï taught: when the Israelites made a covenant *to do* before *hearing*, six hundred thousand angels descended and attached to each Israelite two crowns, one for doing, the other for hearing. . . . Rabbi Eliezer said: "When the Israelites (etc.)... First the doing, then the hearing." (p. 68).

He considers the Revelation to be: "a *Yes* older than naive spontaneity" (p. 106), for the Tora is "an order the self values without having had to enter into it (p. 107). Here again is the voice of the father: "To hear a voice is *ipso facto* to accept the obligation toward he who speaks" (pp. 104-105).

But now we understand that it is not to hear this voice that is fitting, not to understand it, not to obey it as an order, not to submit to it by conquering egotism—all operations that are mediations, requiring mediations, leading to processes (to discourses of process, as Kierkegaard said); this dead voice, this scripture, is not a message, it is a gift, it is the true present as absence, and this gift consists in that, through it, the subject is taken, seized. This is why Levinas can write: "The Tora is given in the light of a face" (*Ibid.*, p. 103). This voice is a light, and the face, *Totality and Infinity* has taught us, is what the invisible lights, the presence of the absolute Other.[12] "Plato has reminded us of the long ordeal of the eye that wants to fix the sun in its abode. But the sun is not forever withdrawn from view. Ths invisible of the Bible is the idea of Good beyond Being."[13] Facing the Odyssey of the eye, that loops its loop in the sun, the disseizure without return.

V

The truly fundamental thesis of *Moses and Monotheism* (1939) is not Moses' Egyptian origin. Freud makes it no secret that he absolutely needs this romantic hypothesis about his hero's birth for his construct.[14] It is indeed on condition that Moses not be Jewish that it will become plausible that the Hebrew people, tired of his domination, put him to death. The essential point for Freud is that Moses should have been assassinated, since it is by this *Agieren*, this *acting-out* (the compulsive murder of the paternal figure repeating in non-recognition that of the primal father thematized in *Totem and Taboo* in 1913) that the Jews escape the general movement of the first murder's recognition and the religion of reconciliation, Christianity, that offers the libido its compromise-formations. For the Jews, the son does not have to ask for and obtain a reconciliation with the father. There is between them an alliance, which is a *pre-conciliation*.[15] The alliance does not belong to the order of a contract; the absolute inequality of the two parties informs it, the son is seized by the father's voice, and what this voice gives is not a heritage, nor a mission, still less a knowledge: this gift is the commandment that the son may be and remain seized by the voice of the father.

> *Ghost:* Adieu, adieu, adieu, remember me. . . .
> *Hamlet:* Now to my word; / It is "Adieu, adieu, remember me." (*Hamlet* I.v.91, 110-111).

This modality of the ascendancy that makes the son remain in absolute inequality before the father, is what the tragedy of Hamlet stages. It must assuredly be said, with Ernest Jones, that

Hamlet's reluctance to avenge his father's murder proceeds from his identification with the murderer, and that Claudius, by the king's assassination and his marriage with the widow, occupies the son's place in the triangle of the Danish family. But what is important is this *displacement* itself, on account of which Hamlet, unlike Oedipus, does *not fulfill* his desire. Hamlet seems to come to Oedipus *after* the latter has manifested itself in the double crime of his uncle. Another has taken both his and his father's place, has exposed the desire in its scandal.

The *Tragedy of Hamlet* thus begins after the end of *Oedipus the King*, and the articulation of the figures of desire to see/know in Freud finds its respondent in that of the figures of desire that western theatre exhibits. The son's displacement by the uncle introduces, in the order of affect, Hamlet's ambivalence with respect to Cornelius; but what is important is that, in the scenic order proper, its is correlative to an essential displacement of the subject in his relation to desire. *Oedipus fulfills his desire in non-recognition; Hamlet un-fulfills his desire in representation.* The complex function of representation in Shakespearian tragedy must be tied to the dimension of non-fulfillment, i.e. to the properly Judaic contribution. Let us attempt to establish these two points; we will perhaps be able to understand why the Danish prince doubles, and what he adds to, the Greek king as a figure of desire in the constitution of psychoanalysis.

First of all, the function of representation. There is, to be sure, the play within the play, the tragedy of Gonzago, that Hamlet stages in order to trap his uncle: ". . . the play's the thing/Wherein I'll catch the conscience of the king" (II.ii.632-633). While he indicates to the actors the way to play their parts, Hamlet forcefully defines the function of the theatre: ". . . the purpose of playing, whose end, both at the first, and now, was and is, to hold, as 'twere the mirror up to nature" (III.ii.21).

(Allow me again to place next to this mirror of the stage that which Freud speaks of in his *Recommendations to Physicians Practising Psychoanalysis* (1912): "The physician should be impenetrable to the patient, and, like a mirror, reflect nothing but what is shown to him.")[16]

Gonzago's tragedy represents Hamlet's, only a slight displacement—the murderer is the nephew of the victim, not his brother—disguises the crudeness of the repetition. Hamlet counts on the tragic effect of recognition to catch Claudius out. Thus the theatre itself is going to fill on stage a function comparable to that filled by the prophet Tiresias in *Oedipus*. The king of Thebes was an innocent criminal; he had to encounter the truth, being unable to recognize it. But since the end of Olympus, the parricidal (fratricidal) and incestuous are no longer innocent, they are "cognizant" of their crime, they are able to "recognize" it when it is represented.

The play within the play gives, so to speak, the manifest function of representation:

$$\text{Gonzago} \underset{\text{Nephew}}{\overline{}} \text{Queen} \qquad = \qquad \text{King} \underset{\text{Claudius}}{\overline{}} \text{Gertrude}$$

Its latent function is elsewhere. There is another duplication, another specular presentation in the Shakespearian tragedy. The subject ensnared in it is no longer Claudius, but Hamlet himself. There are two families in play on the Shakespearean stage: Hamletid and Polonid. The Oedipal triangle is replicated here in the following way:

$$\text{Dead King} \underset{\text{Hamlet}}{\overline{}} \text{Gertrude} \qquad = \qquad \text{King} \underset{\text{Laertes}}{\overline{}} \text{Gertrude}$$

Between these two sets are two main modalities of relation: that of the spectacle, the mirror with its ambivalence; that of *acting-out*. Their examination will permit comprehension of the displacement of Ophelia onto the position that Gertrude occupies. One may note right away that Polonius' wife is never mentioned in the play, except in one passage, which I leave the reader to judge: Laertes, enraged by his father's death, replies to Claudius who wants to calm him: "That drop of blood that's calm proclaims me bastard/Cries cuckold to my father; brands the harlot/Even here between the chaste unsmirched brow/Of my true mother" (IV.v.117-120).

Speaking of Laertes, Hamlet says: "For by the image of my cause I see/The portraiture of his. . . ." (V.ii.77-78). For Hamlet, Laertes stands as a self representation: a father to avenge; a woman of his blood rendered "mad," "seduced," to restore to her honor, that is, to her place. Like the prince, Laertes finds himself before the scandal of desire. But Hamlet sounds Laertes as a model: he recognizes himself in the same place, but does not affectively identify with him. Laertes, in anger and indignation, fulfills without hesitation his debt of death and honor. We know why: the father's murderer and Ophelia's seducer is not a man of the family, is not a paternal figure with which he can identify. Here we encounter the difference that, with repetition, gives representation—a function of recognition in distancing. During the duel in Act V, that opposes him to Laertes, Hamlet declares: "I'll be your foil, Laertes" (V.ii.266). This *foil* is at one and the same time the sword and the setoff: "anything that sets something off by contrast," says the *Concise Oxford Dictionary*. "I will be your foil-*sword*" announces the exchange of swords in the course of combat, the exchange of poison one of them carries, the exchange of death: my death will be your death, a classical relation with the Double. But "I will be your foil-*contrast*" says, it seems to me: you fulfill the debt of vengeance, I unfulfill it, I watch you fulfill it. Instead of acting on the Hamletids' stage, I watch you act on that of the Polonids. The representative distance relieves the pressure of the debt. Here one is close to the articulation of non-fulfillment with representation.

But that is not all. The two triangles communicate not by representation, but by *Agieren*. Hamlet plays an important role on the stage of the Polonids: he kills the father, he estranges the daughter. This role is exactly symmetrical to that performed by the uncle on the stage of the Hamletids. But here the mirror (polonid) does not send back the image: not for a second does Hamlet see himself as the father's assassin and the woman's seducer. When he intervenes on the stage of the Polonids, it is as *another*. And he "knows" it, that is to say, he maintains his identification with Laertes and continues to know nothing of his identification with Claudius, with the father's murderer:

> Was't Hamlet wrong'd Laertes? Never Hamlet:
> If Hamlet from himself be ta'en away,
> And when he's not himself does wrong Laertes,
> Then Hamlet does it not, Hamlet denies it.
> (V.ii.244-247).

How heavy the argumentation of this denial. And the other, the unjust one, "Who does it then?", has no name: "his madness."

We, however, *are* aware of him. The dagger thrust into the drapery (pardi!) has pierced Polonius *in place of* Claudius; the seduction-castration of Ophelia has *replaced* that of which Hamlet's mother was nearly the victim. Hamlet has accomplished his desire, but outside, on the stage of the Polonids. This stage is *another scene*, in that he is missing himself there where he is (in Claudius), and attempts to recognize himself in a place where he is not (in Laertes). Hamlet's desire is unfulfilled on the royal stage, it is *acted-out (agierte)* on this other stage. The two triangles are articulated then in this manner:

Claudius (King) ⎯⊤⎯ Gertrude
      Hamlet (Polonius) ⎯⊤⎯ Ophelia
              ⌊ Laertes

Whether it is a matter of Gonzago's tragedy or of that of the Polonids, the function assigned to representation remains that of recognition. Its principle is that, in the playing of desire's figure, the subject in the audience recognizes his fate, recognizes his lack of recognition. This principle, applied by Hamlet upon the stage, obtains the expected effect on the spectator Claudius. But Hamlet himself, spectator of the other scene (polonid), does not recognize his fate, his non-recognition, except negatively, as his own coldness of feeling, slowness, inertia, as his own lag behind the time prescribed for vengeance, compared to the violence of Laertes. All this scene shows him of himself is therefore his non-fulfillment as a son; what it hides from him is precisely his rootedness in the son's position, in "filial passivity."

Before examining this articulation with desire, one more word on the specificity of representation in *Hamlet*.

I've presented theatre as the reversal of figural (phantastic) space onto the (formally analogous) space of representation. *Hamlet* responds to this reversal a first time: Shakespeare represents his own phantastic space on the stage of the Globe, and thus affords it recognition. The play responds to it a second time: Hamlet, by putting Gonzago on stage, overturns and presents for recognition the Oedipal figure that inhabits Claudius. But the third stage (polonid) does not perform this function, it is not representative, it does not act as a mirror: Hamlet's vision as a spectator is obnubilated once and for all by a blind spot. What this scene offers Hamlet is an alibi: I am Laertes (= I am not Claudius), I must still fulfill the paternal word (= I haven't already fulfilled it by killing Polonius). A scene produced by a parricidal or an incestuous compulsion foreclosed; the stage manager is Hamlet's fate, which is to be unable to fulfill the paternal order, to be unable to take the place of the father, to remain disseized, irreconcilable. Thus on the Shakespearean stage, next to the Italian stage (Gonzago), which is homologous to the preceeding one, there is an entirely other scene where the tragic reversal is itself reversed. This scene is thus a direct exteriorisation unelaborated by the double theatrical reversal, it is the direct externalization of the Hamletian fate: in short a scene that is a symptom. But it is due to the Shakespearean cast of these different scenes that *we* in the audience are able to see the blind spot, to see Hamlet not see, and that Freud can begin to perceive what the other scene is, the unconscious, and to point to neurosis as the impossibility of re-presentation.

Now the other point, the relation between non-fulfillment and this complex function of representation? First we must understand this non-fulfillment. Oedipus fulfills his desire, he takes the place of his father; his desire and his fate coincide. For Hamlet, the father's place is taken, and the paternal order is to leave it vacant; this vacancy can only be obtained by suppressing the usurper; but the latter is for Hamlet a paternal figure. The formula of Hamlet's desire is: kill your father; the formula of his fate, of his debt is: kill his simulacrum. He will kill a simulacrum of a simulacrum, Polonius, further removed from the paternal figure than Claudius (as indicates the configuration of the polonid family, in particular the relation Polonius-Ophelia). There is a non-fulfillment of desire and a fulfillment of fate. There is fulfillment of non-fulfillment. This is the configuration of the *Agieren*, that effectuates desire without fulfilling it, outside its scene, on an alibi stage set up by derivation and without re-presentation.

Such is precisely also the configuration of the rejection that, according to Freud, blocks the road of anamnesis for the Jews: just as Hamlet by killing Polonius on the other stage will fail to recognize his parricidal desire and remain seized by the task intimated by the voice, in the same way the Hebrew people—by killing Moses in an *acting-out*—foregoes recognizing itself as the father's murderer and cuts off the path of reconciliation, the one traced by the desire to see: the Christian path that announces at its end the vision of the father. It is not I, Hamlet, (it is Claudius) who has killed my father; my father speaks to me, has chosen me; all those who appear as figures of the father are usurpers: Claudius, Polonius (Hamlet). . . . Cognition is the usurpation by the self of the position of the Word. I am and remain the absolute son, the passivity, which is the Good. Egoism, the heroism of the self whose model is Laertes (and Claudius himself) (and Oedipus), is renounced on the manifest level.

If such is indeed the difference between *Oedipus* and *Hamlet*, a difference between the representation of desire fulfilling itself in non-recognition and that of desire non-fulfilling itself in compulsive representation, a difference between Greek fate (Apollo is not a paternal voice) and Jewish kerygma, one can perhaps begin to understand the articulation of the figures disclosed by Starobinski. To understand as well what, on a day of anger, Freud wrote to Pfarrer Pfister, whom he had just violently accused of knowing nothing of the sexual theory of neuroses:

> I can only envy you, from a therapeutic point of view, the possibility of sublimation in religion. But what is fine in religion certainly does not belong to psychoanalysis. It is normal that in therapeutic matters our paths should separate here and so they may remain. Quite in passing, why was psychoanalysis not created by one of all the pious men: why was it for an entirely atheist Jew that one waited?[17]

It was necessary to wait for it to be a Jew because it had to be someone for whom religious reconciliation ("sublimation") was prohibited, for whom art, re-presentation itself, was unable to fill the Greek function of truth; it was necessary *to wait*, because it was necessary that this someone belong to a people for whom the beginning is the end of Oedipus and the end of the theatre; a people who has renounced the desire to see to the point that it wants to *do* before it wants to *hear* (because there is still too much seeing in hearing).

And it was necessary that this Jew be an atheist in order that the renounced desire to see could change into a desire to know; it was necessary that the staging, this opening of the secondary space to the primary process, could give place to the analogous opening that the double rule of free association and free-floating attention hollows out; but in discourse alone, its back turned, without looking, without even the third eye, with only the third ear: the ear that wants to hear *what* the voice of the Other says, instead of being seized and dispossessed, and this is the atheism demanded by Freud.

Translated by Susan Hanson

Notes

[1] [Chapter VI of *The Interpretation of Dreams*, defines "dream thoughts" as what is "between the manifest content of dreams and the conclusions of our enquiry: namely their *latent* content. . . ," (*Standard Edition*, IV, London: Hogarth Press, 1966) p. 277.]

[2] A. Green, *Un oeil en trop, le complexe d'Oedipe dans la tragédie* (Paris: Editions de Minuit, collection "Critique," 1969), p. 41.

[3] J. Laplanche, "Interpréter [avec] Freud," *L'Arc*, 34 (1968), p. 39.

[4] [J. Starobinski's "Introduction" to the French translation of E. Jones' *Hamlet and Oedipus*, appears only in the French edition, (Paris: Gallimard, 1967, translated by A.-M. LeGoll).]

[5] A. Green p.280ff. I will separate here from Green on a specific point: it seems to me that he does not give the *reversal of spaces* its true place, which is that of the theatre and of art in general. His model of a double overturning, borrowed from the theory of narcissism and masochism, does not account for the *truth function* of representation.

[6] T. Reik, *Listening with the Third Ear* (New York: Farrar, Strauss, 1948).

[7] R. Bultmann, *Das Urchristentum in Rahmen der antiken Religionen* (Zurich: Artemis-Verlag, 1949); [*Primitive Christianity in its Contemporary Setting*, translated by R.H. Fuller (New York: Meridian Books, 1959), my translation.]

[8] E. Levinas, *Quatre lectures talmudiques* (Paris: Editions de Minuit, 1968), p. 130.

[9] E. Levinas, "Humanisme et anarchie," *Revue internationale de philosophie*, 85-86 (1968), p. 335.

[10] [Although *après-coup* is usually translated by *deferred action*, *after the event* would be more appropriate here. It is the French term for the German *Nachträglichkeit* which Freud used extensively and that is essential to his understanding of the unconscious and of psychic reality. The English reader may find it useful to refer to "French Freud," *Yale French Studies*, 48 (1972),

which gives access to French texts not elsewhere translated into English, also to J. Laplanche and J.-B. Pontalis' *The Language of Psycho-analysis*, translated by Donald Nicholson-Smith (New York: Norton & Company, Inc., 1973).]

¹¹Freud, "Creative Writers and Day-Dreaming," *Standard Edition*, IX, pp. 149-150.

¹²E. Levinas, *Totalité et infini* (La Haye: Martinus Nyhoff, 1974); *Totality and Infinity*, translated by Alphonso Linguis (Pittsburgh: Duquesne University Press, 1969), my translation.

¹³E. Levinas, "Humanisme et anarchie," pp. 333-334.

¹⁴Freud, *Standard Edition*, XXIII, p. 89.

¹⁵It could be shown, contrary to Freud's construct in *Moses and Monotheism*, that this figure corresponds to a mode of rejection that is not a repression, but a foreclosure.

¹⁶[Freud, *Standard Edition*, XII, p. 118.]

¹⁷Letter of October 9, 1918, *Psychoanalysis and faith: the letters of Sigmund Freud and Oskar Pfister*, translated by Erich Mosbacher (New York: Basic Books, c. 1963), my translation.

The Connivances of Desire with the Figural

The hypothesis which guides Freud in understanding the dreamwork is a radical connivance between the figure and desire. It allows him to establish a strong link between the order of desire and that of the figural through the category of transgression: the "text" of the preconscious (day's residues, memory-traces) undergoes disruptions which make it unrecognizable, illegible; the deep matrix in which desire is caught thrives on this illegibility: it expresses itself in disordered forms and hallucinatory images.

Let us examine this machinery. Three kinds of components may be distinguished. The *image-figure* I see in hallucinations or dreams, the one paintings or films present, is an object set at a distance, a theme. It belongs to the visible order; it is a revealing "trace." The *form-figure* is present in the perceptible, it may even be visible, but is in general not seen: André Lhote calls it "tracé regulateur," the Gestalt of a configuration, the architecture of a painting, in short, the schema. The *matrix-figure* is invisible in principle, subject to primal repression, immediately intermixed with discourse, primal phantasy. It is nonetheless a figure, not a structure, because it consists in a violation of discursive order from the outset, in a violence done to the transformations that this order authorizes. It cannot be intelligibly apprehended, for this very apprehension would make its immersion in the unconscious unintelligible. This immersion attests, however, that what is in question is inded the "other" of discourse and intelligibility. To establish the *matrix-figure* in a textual, *a fortiori* systematic space would be to imagine it as an $\alpha\rho\chi\acute{\eta}$, to entertain a double phantasy: first that of an origin, and then that of an utterable origin, demonstrates to the contrary, that our origin is an absence of origin and that everything that appears as the object of a primal discourse is an hallucinatory *image-figure*, located precisely in this initial non-locus.

Image, form and matrix are figures in as much as each one of them belongs to the space of the figural according to a strict articulation specific to each one. Freud's energetic model of the reflex apparatus helps us understand this articulation. The economic hypothesis he derived from this was that all unpleasure is a charge, all pleasure a discharge. Pleasure obeys the principle according to which the discharge of energy is always sought through the most expeditious means: the aim is to return the psychical apparatus to a state of minimal excitation.[1] According to this principle, energy circulates freely within the psychical system, ready to be cathected into this or that zone, indifferently, as long as the zone offers the possibility of a discharge. This property of processes subject to the pleasure principle reveals the unbound character of the energy it uses. On the contrary, when the expenditure of energy is subordinated to the reality principle, the function it obeys is no longer to cancel all tension, but to maintain energy at a constant level; and more importantly still, the discharge cannot take place in just any zone of the psychical apparatus: some of these zones are open to others through facilitation but others are isolated by obstacles and the whole set of bindings regulating associations and exclusions is controlled by the Ego. The principle of this reality subordinates the possibility of a discharge to the transformation of the relationship between the apparatus and the external world, through the use of language, through motor activity, or both. Starting from perceptions and memory of perceptions, through word-presentations, the flow of energy moves toward the centers and organs of motor activity; Freud calls this the "progressive" path.[2]

Guided by Fechner's psycho-analysis model as it might be, this description nevertheless already contains, metaphorically, a theme never to be disavowed and which is essential to the location of the figural. The space in which energy moves is qualitatively different, according as it is free or bound. The space of pleasure and that of reality are not the same. This already appears in Freud's analysis of the infantile condition—which is and remains the adult's condition. When faced by an "internal" stimulus, before the secondary process is established and thus does not yet allow the modification of the outer world necessary for the discharge to occur, the subject is in a state of "motorische Hilflosigkeit," of motor helplessness:[3] in the absence of the specific action[4] whose performance would relieve the pressure of the need, the satisfaction of this need is entirely dependent on an external person. Three givens will thus be disassociated: the motor component of the reflex movement, e.g. the sucking accompanying the discharge; the affective component of satisfaction; the sensory component of the object whose intercession suppresses anxiety and permits the discharge. "The first wishing seems to have been a hallucinatory cathecting of the memory of satisfaction."[5] Desire thus is born through "anaclisis" (attachment);[6] sexuality as a search for pleasure is buttressed by the instinct of self-preservation, which can be satisfied only through the specific action of a specific organ; it grasps the instinctual aim (satisfaction) and its object (the organ of the specific action) as the means of pleasure. Desire develops as a power for pleasure disconnected from the satisfaction of need.

Wish fulfillment (Wunscherfüllung) contains in itself the absence of its object. Essential to desire, this absence is constitutive of its relation to any object which claims to be *its* object. Likewise, one could say that the "absence" of the organ is what characterizes desire's use of the body: organs are not seen by desire as a means to satisfy the need, but as erogenous zones whose excitation induces the staging of phantasy. The body is thus diverted. It is also fragmented: in self-preservation, the specific function is in principle subordinated to the survival of the organism as a whole; for desire, every organ is a possible erogenous zone, cathecting the organ becomes an end in itself if it provides for the production of the phantasies which fulfil desire. The disruption of realist and biological space which accompanies anaclisis is thus obvious.

Freud gives us an idea of this upheaval when he stresses the importance of regression.[7] Hallucinatory fulfillment is regressive in three ways: first, because it takes the retrogressive course of the psychical apparatus, contrary to what happens in specific action. Action starts from the excitation, goes through memory-traces, verbal traces, the motor zones, produces a transformation of reality and finally provides satisfaction as an outward discharge. In the fulfillment of desire, excitation passes through the different layers of the apparatus in the reverse direction and cathects perceptual memories with such an intensity that it induces the hallucination. The displacement of energy towards the perceptual end instead of the verbal-motor end is therefore regressive. This regression is the result of the principle of the immediate discharge at the lowest possible cost, or Nirvana principle. But regression also takes place in an historical sense, because the memory of the first satisfaction is reactivated like a return to the infantile experience. And above all, regression is characterized by the use of "primitive methods of expression and representation in place of the usual ones;"[8] "We call it regression when in a dream, an idea is turned back into the sensory image from which it was originally derived."[9] There is an "attraction which memories couched in visual form exert over thoughts separated from consciousness."[10] Regression is produced as much by this as by the complementary action of censorship. What is at work is the elaboration of disfigured figures in place of recognizable figures, of rebuses in place of texts, is not only prohibition, but also desire's own force operating in its distinctive space and according to its specific relation with representation. Here, the figural is understood as the antipode of the verbal and the motor, i.e. of the reality principle with its two functions, language and action. To these two functions, desire turns its back.

This very "otherness" is also the subject of an analysis subsequently carried out in order to characterize the unconscious;[11] Freud attempts to make the unconscious space intelligible by continually contrasting it with the space where processes under preconscious control are produced. The four characteristics he retains are: first of all, the absence of "negations, of doubts, of degrees of certainty" or "the absence of contradictions;"[12]

unconscious "judgements" have no modality and no quality, they are always assertive and positive. Secondly, "the cathecting intensities (in the Ucs) are much more mobile:"[13] the unbound character of energy characterizes what Freud calls the primary process; the "free" movements of this energy, he says, are displacement and condensation. These operations are explicitly held to impede the secondary process, i.e. perception, motility and *articulated language*. The third feature of the unconscious processes is that they are "timeless; i.e. they are not ordered temporally, are not altered by the passing of time; they have no reference to time at all."[14] Finally, the unconscious processes "pay just as little regard to reality," they are subject to the pleasure principle, to the "substitution of psychical reality for external reality."[15] As a result, these processes not only do not enter into the categories of judgement (modality, quality) but they do not even obey the fundamental constraints of discourse: condensation violates lexical constraints, displacement and the disregard for temporality violate the constraints of syntax. As for indifference to reality, it manifests both a refusal to consider (linguistic) reference and a disdain for the dimension of designation. Unconscious processes transgress the two spaces of discourse, i.e. that of the system and that of reference. The space which contains them and that they themselves produce is then another space, differing from that of the system in that it is incessant mobility and from that of reference in its treating words like things. Mobility in the systematic field of language and of the order of discourse short-circuits sense and introduces "non-sense;" transgression of the referential distance leads back to magic, to "the omnipotence of thought." There is thus a violation of both negations; of the negativity which separates the terms of the system, and of that which keeps the object of discourse at a variable distance.

One can see that it is not enough to say that the unconscious is the introduction of the second negativity, as variability, into the first one. Such a reflection might lead us to contrast the philosophy of the system with the philosophy of phenomenological "gesture," of chiasma, of depth. But fundamentally, the unconscious space is no more that of gesture than it is that of the invariables. It is a topological space. If one can mistake its effects, it is because, from the point of view of language, transgression of the space of the system by displacements and condensations can be attributed as well to the characteristic mobility of the referential (sensory) space as to the mobility of the primary process. The overlapping of these two functions may not be itself innocent. The force moving at full speed within the wild space of the unbound can pass itself off as the gracious and spacious mobility of the gestating gesture of phenomenologies. What could cause confusion yet at the same time obliging us to be on our guard is that the dream operations comprise not only distortion, condensing and displacing the dream elements, but also the considerations of representability. Isn't this the proof that we have to deal with the dimension of designation? That this very dimension, mapped back into the course of discourse and onto the temperate and well-regulated space of communication, is what induces turbulences, sense effects which do not proceed from signification nor from syntax, but from vision?

If we stop here, we will perhaps develop a philosophy of the subject, we will become incapable of understanding dreams and the symptom in general. It is not the aesthetic space which comes to superimpose itself on the linguistic space in the dream; the bodily reach itself is, so to speak, enlarged beyond its worldly limits of the waking state. We must really take into consideration that we *sleep* while dreaming and that it is precisely the connaturality of the body and the world which is suspended by an immobility that not only eliminates the world, but also has the effect of mistaking the body for the world,[16] and, more importantly still, that the figures produced within this world which takes over the expanding stage of the body are not in the least governed by the rules of connaturality, by the directions of perceptual space, by the constitution of depth which makes "real" things out of signs that afford one of their sides while masking the others. In dreams and neurotic symptoms, these properties of worldly figures disappear. When Freud teaches us that one of the essential operations of the dream is representation, let us therefore be on our guard: we must conclude from this that we have left the realm of language; but we must also assume—if it is true that the figure offered by the dream is not *bound* any more to the constraints of designation (which include both variability of the point of view and unilaterality of the visible), than it is to those of language—that we are no longer in the referential or worldly dimension. What we are dealing with is indeed a representation, but the rules of this scenic space are no longer those of sensory space. It is not only the author's text which is cut, superimposed, scrambled, it is also the face of the actors, the place where they stand, their clothing, their identity; as to the sets, they change in the middle of the action without warning. Action itself has no unity.

We can now come back to the classification of our figures and attempt to specify their respective connection with unconscious space. The *image-figure* is that made visible on the oneiric or quasi-oneiric stage. What is infringed here is the set of rules regulating the constitution of the perceived object. The *image-figure* deconstructs the percept, it produces itself within a space of difference. It can be precisely defined: deconstructing the outline of the silhouette, the *image-figure* is the transgression of the revealing trace.

Pablo Picasso, *Etude de nu*, 1941, Galerie Louise Leiris, graphite, reproduced from Pierre Francastel, *Peinture et société*, Paris, Gallimard, 1965.

This is conclusively illustrated in Picasso's sketch (Fig. 1), where the object of deconstruction is the edge, the line which shows that there is a single and reifying point of view; the coexistence of several countours infers the simultaneity of several points of view. The scene where this woman is sleeping does not belong to "real" space, it allows several positions of the same body in the same place and at the same time. Erotic indifference to time, to reality, to exclusive poses. Similar examples of the deconstruction of values and colors could be found.

The *form-figure* is that which supports the visible without being seen, its nervure; it can itself be made visible, however. Its relation to unconscious space is given by the transgression of the *good form* (Gestalt). This "good form" is the Pythagorean and neoplatonic form, grounded in a tradition of Euclidean geometry. A philosophy, nay a mystique, of the number and of its luminous, cosmic value depends upon it.[17] This form is Apollinian. Unlike it, the unconscious *form-figure*, form as a figural form, would be anti-Gestalt, a "bad form." We could call it Dionysian,[18] as an energetics indifferent to the unity of the whole.

It is certainly difficult to find examples of this in art, since art, we are told, demands that Apollo cooperate with Dionysius. Pollock's "action painting," at least in the works produced from 1946 to 1953, where the method of dripping (that we call "passion painting") was uncompromisingly pushed to its limits, could give us an idea of what the "bad form" might be like. A plastic screen entirely covered with chromatic flows, no stroke, not even a "trace," no effects of echo or rhythm coming from the repetition or reentry of forms, values or colours on the surface of the painting, thus no recognizable figure; all of this suggests that we have passed over to the side of Bacchic delirium, descended unto the substratum where the plastic "invariables," the linear invariable at least, become a whirlwind, where energy circulates at top speed from one point of the pictorial space to another, prohibiting the eye from resting anywhere, from investing here or there, be it only for a second, its phantasmagoric charge.[19]

Finally, the *matrix-figure*. Not only is this not seen, it is no more visible than it is legible. It does not belong to plastic space any more than it does to textual space. It is difference itself, and as such, does not allow the minimal amount of structural polarity which its verbalization would require, or the minimal amount of construction without which its plastic expression as image or form cannot be obtained. Discourse, image and form are all expression as image or form cannot be obtained. Discourse, image and form Discourse, image and form are all unequal to it, for it resides in all three spaces together. Anyone's works are never but the derivatives of this matrix; we might perhaps catch a fleeting glimpse of it through their superimposition.[20] But the confusion of the spaces that prevails originally is such that words are being treated as things and as forms, things as forms or words, forms as words or as things, deconstruction bears no longer only on the textual trace as in the figural image, or on the regulating trace as in the figural form, but on the very locus of the matrix, which belongs at the same time to the space of the text, to that of the scenario, and to that of the stage: graphy, geometry, representation—each one deconstructed on account of the other two's unexpected mixture. Freud should be closely followed here.

Such are thus the fundamental modes of the connivance that desire establishes with figurality: transgression of the object, transgression of form, transgression of space.

Translated by Anne Knab

Notes

[1] It will be shown in *Beyond the Pleasure Principle* (1920; Standard Edition, XVIII, p. 7), that the functioning outlined here combines two principles: inertia or Nirvana and constancy, Eros being involved with the death instinct on one hand and reality on the other.

[2] This very rough outline corresponds to *A Project for a Scientific Psychology* (1895; see *The Origins of Psycho-Analysis*, Standard Edition, I) and to *The Interpretation of Dreams* (1900;

Standard Edition, IV-V), chapter VII, sections B) and C).

[3] *Inhibitions, Symptoms and Anxiety* (1926; Standard Edition, XX, p. 167).

[4] *Three Essays on the Theory of Sexuality* (1905; Standard Edition, VII, p. 135).

[5] *The Interpretation of Dreams, loc. cit.*, p. 598.

[6] *Anlehnung*. See mainly *Three Essays on the Theory of Sexuality, loc. cit.*, pp. 181-82, 222-30. This concept was developed by Laplanche and Pontalis in the article "Anaclisis," *The Language of Psycho-Analysis*, London, Hogarth Press and the Institute of Psycho-Analysis, 1973 (translated from the French by Donald Nicholson Smith).

[7] See in particular *The Interpretation of Dreams, loc. cit.*, sec. B.

[8] *Ibid.*, p. 548.

[9] *Ibid.*, p. 544.

[10] *Ibid.*, p. 547.

[11] *The Unconscious*, (1915; Standard Edition, XIV, p. 196).

[12] *Ibid.*, p. 186. In the same way, one finds in *New Introductory Lectures on Psycho-Analysis* the following: "All the linguistic instruments by which we express the subtler relations of thought—the conjunction and prepositions, the changes in declension and conjugation—are dropped, because there are no means of representing them, just as in a primitive language without any grammar, only the raw material of thought is expressed and abstract terms are taken back to the concrete ones that are at their basis." (1932; Standard Edition XXII, p. 20).

[13] *Ibid.*, p. 186.

[14] *Ibid.*, p. 187.

[15] *Ibid.*, p. 187

[16] M. Sami-Ali, "Préliminaire d'une théorie psychanalytique de l'espace imaginaire," *Revue francaise de psychanalyse*, XXXIII (janvier/février 1969).

[17] That which is found in Matila C. Ghyka's book, *Le nombre d'or*, Paris, Gallimard, 1931; and in Lhote's philosophy of plastic art.

¹⁸ See A. Ehrenzweig, *The Psycho-Analysis of Artistic Vision and Hearing, An Introduction to a Theory of Unconscious Perceptions*, London, Routledge and Kegan Paul, 1953, p. 57 and following.

¹⁹ In saying this, I draw away from Italo Tomassoni's phenomenologico-existential interpretation of Pollock's work (*Pollock*, Florence, Sadea, 1968). I believe André Breton's position was more accurate when he wrote about Archile Gorky, an artist very close to Pollock from the very beginning of their respective works: "I say that the eye is not *open* as long as it plays only the passive role of a mirror, even if the water of this mirror offers some interesting particularity: exceptionally limpid or sparkling, or bubbling or facetted; - that I deem this eye just as dead as that of slaughtered bulls if it is only capable of *reflecting*, whether it reflects the object under one or several of its angles, at rest or in motion, whether this object belongs to the waking world or to the realm of dreams. The eye's treasure is elsewhere: most artists are still turning the face of the watch in all directions; they have not the slightest idea of the spring hidden in the opacous case./ The spring of the eye... Archile Gorky is for me the first painter to whom this secret has been completely revealed. The eye's ultimate function cannot be to inventory as does the bailiff's visual organ, or to delight in the illusions of *fausse reconnaissance*, as does the oculus of maniacs." (*Le surréalisme et la peinture*, Paris, Gallimard, 1965), pp. 196-197). One must note the total difference of function existing between a painting in which the *figural-form* is displayed and another that exhibits the *figural-image*. The two spaces are not compatible. The space of Picasso's sketch remains acceptable, even likable; it is the imaginary space, and although torn from the silence of the individual psyche and thrown under our collective eyes, it allows desire's fulfillment for the object (be it deconstructed) is still offered on the representational stage. Pollock's formal or rather anti-formal chromatic flows, on the other hand, reveal the movement of desire itself, instead of its hallucinatory object; they cannot be cathected by the pleasure principle for desire does not wish to see but to lose itself through a

discharge upon and within the object. Pollock's space is one of maximal charge; no loss can be envisaged because there is no objectivist or gestaltist exit. From surrealism to the American lyric abstract trend that followed the war, what one witnesses is precisely a reversal of the *figural-image* into the *figural-form*; deconstructive activity ceases from attacking only visible outlines and superimposing visionary contours onto them, it attempts to break up the very space of mise-en-scène, the regulating trace, the spring of the eye. Dali embodies the obstinate preservation of scenic space, while with Matta, Gorky, Pollock, the probing and the exhibition of its substratum begin. A. Breton had foreseen this: "Matta carries the disintegration of external aspects much further, for to those who can see, all these aspects are open, open not only as Cézanne's apple is to light, but to everything else, including *other opaque bodies*; they are always ready to fuse and only in this fusion can the golden key to life be forged [...]. It is also thus that he unceasingly invites us to a *new space*, deliberately wrenched from the old one, since the latter makes sense only insofar as it is distributive of elementary and closed bodies." (*Le surréalisme et la peinture, loc. cit.*, pp. 192-93).

[20] This is the method advocated by Charles Mauron in *Des métaphores obsédantes au mythe personnel*, Paris, Corti, 1963. Possibility of the incompossibles, occupation of a single space by several bodies or of a single body by several positions, simultaneity of the successive, consequently, approach of a timelessness which will be the chronical pendant of this "topological" space. But in this particular case, Picasso is satisfied with deconstructing profiles, the revealing trace. Compare with Paul Klee's *Der L. Platz im Bau* (water-colour and ink on paper—G. David Thompson, Pittsburgh), where the incompossibles are not of the same rank, some of them belonging, as here, to the *image-figure* (revealing traces) while others relate to the *form-figure* (regulating traces). The "Zwischenwelt" takes place beyond the sketch. The sketch, as in Picasso's drawing, refers to the phenomenology of perception; Klee's sketches and watercolours bear upon the economics of sensory possibility.

Notes on the Critical Function
of the Work of Art

[*The student committee in charge of the Humanities House at the University of Paris at Nanterre, in March 1979, took the initiative in setting up a group of talk-debates on the theme* Art and Society: *Pierre Gaudibert and I opened it with a discussion entitled "Art, Ideology, Phantasy." The following notes come from my contribution to that discussion.*]

I would like to begin by recalling that, throughout his work, Freud defined "reality" as a bound set of perceptions that can be verified through activities of transformation and signified in bound sets of words, i.e. verbalized.

In fact, the criteria of reality are those of communication—objects are real to the extent that they are communicable on two levels: on the level of language and on that of practice. It is obvious, although not always explicitly stated, that Freud considers reality to be fundamentally social, while he at the same time always keeps it in quotation marks. This reality is the little, even the very little "reality." Which means that this bound set of perceptions, signifiable in words, exchangeable by gestures, has gaps, is lacunary; there are regions that remain outside reach, that cannot be approached, that are utterly unrecognized. There are words that are unpronounceable because they lack "signification," perceptions that are impossible, things that cannot be seen: thus, there are screens. This is the aspect I would call "Dada-reality": reality insofar as the fabric that holds it together is missing. It is obviously in these regions where something is lacking, either the transformative experience or the words to exchange (because they are impossible to say), that works of art can take place. Figures, in Freudian terms, (not only image-figures in the plastic sense, but also three or one-dimensional figures; a movement can be a figure, so can a music)—that is to say objects that do not exist according to the two criteria just stated, that are not transformable, or at least whose reality is not measurable by their transformability—are essentially not linguistically communicable. (The commonplaces I am running through rapidly underlie Freud's characterization of dreams and the primary process, even if they are not explicitly stated.) These objects can be characterized as figures precisely to the extent that they belong to an order of sense—to an order of existence—which is neither that of language, nor of practical transformation. I tentatively suggest calling this order an order of figure, not in the sense of figurative, but in a sense I would like to call figural. What seems important to me is that this figural object—whether it be music or painting—not be posed as an object of perception or as a text, not be presented as an object transformable by practical activity, nor as an object communicable in language, as discourse. When these figural sets are posed as real objects, then what one is dealing with is a completely different phenomenon, for example a dream or an hallucination; what I mean is that there are indeed border-line cases in which I can believe the scene I see is a stage upon which I could modify these object-relations, or else that the voices I hear issue from persons who are speaking to me, and with whom I could engage in a dialogue. What we are dealing with here are hallucinative misapprehension phenomena. But the work of art never exists in this form, the figural work never consists in forms whose existence we are going to be mistaken about. Which means that these sense formations are effectively present in the gaps of reality, if one can so speak, precisely in places where the testing of reality through its practical transformation, hence its verbalized signification, do not intervene. It is essential to figural reality that it not be posed as pure and simple reality. Indeed, it would almost suffice to say that when a figural reality is presented as plain reality, i.e. as communicable, signifiable, and verbalizable, one is dealing with an ideology in the Marxist sense of the term; when figural reality is given as something other than what it is, when it is given as reality, one can speak of ideology in so far as the fulfillment of desire is functioning. It is obvious that the image—notably in cinema—most often does not function as an image, i.e. as something that belongs to this sort of intermediary scene and sense that are not the real scene or the actual sense of reality, but that it begins to function as a scene in which my desire is caught and comes to fulfillment. This can happen, for example, in the form of a projection into the characters or the situations staged by cinema or, in the case of so-called erotic images, to the extent that the roles presented can directly find a place in my own phantasizing or yet again, more subtly, when the film's cutting and editing as well catch my desire in their net, also fulfilling it, no longer from the point of view of the image itself, but through the organization of the narrative.

II

In a society reputed to be archaic, there is a certain function of art that is, in fact, a religious function in the strict sense of the term; art, in this case, belongs to the society's system of self-integration: it is an integral part of the system. One could say, moreover, that the culture of this society is also simply an art. It functions as a religion, as something that joins people by permitting them to communicate. In this society, communication does not operate according to the criteria given by Freud and also by Marx—the criteria of practical transformation and verbalization—but through forms—plastic, architectural—and through rhythms that allow a "communication" of sorts on the level of the individual unconscious. What one is dealing with is an art-society; this was art's mode of existence for millenia. It can be said that, until the nineteenth century, entire regions of modern society, the peasantry and even the proletariat, continued to function in this way. This kind of art has become impossible. Hegel, who already knew this, used to say that, for us, art is dead, and the time of aesthetics has come. Duchamp as well, and much more radically! There is a problem Duchamp said, of anti-art, a-art, that is to say, non-art. This means that the integrative function of art, the possibility of communicating outside the modes that are language and practical activity, has disappeared in our society because figural forms have been destroyed by the system which has predominated in the West from the nineteenth century on; these figural forms could not resist the requirements of the reproduction of capital. In this sense, religion has been destroyed, and its forms of coexistence, its communications through figures, have become impossible. Attempting to reconstitute such forms is futile. Primitive culture cannot be invented; it is *given* by definition, which means that, even in a revolutionized and revolutionary society, man's type of coexistence could not have primitive society as its model. The function of a revolutionary art is thus very precisely determined. What art does—what it ought to do—is always to unmask all attempts to reconstitute a pseudo-religion; in other words, every time the reconstitution of a kind of writing, a "graphy"—a set of forms that produces a psychic resonance and reproduces itself—is undertaken, the function of anti-art is to unmask it as ideological; in the Marxist sense of the term, to unmask it as an endeavor to make us believe that there are in our societies "primary" modes of communication of this type, which is not true. This was one of the functions of Pop art, at least in some cases: to take objects that look real, objects about which people are in agreement, that they value, through which they communicate, advertising posters or cars, for example—and to deconstruct them. To take these objects that are the objects of the social reality in which we find ourselves and to meticulously paint them in a realist way, but on a two-dimensional screen. To represent a car in this fashion, for example, is already a deconstruction, for in this mode of representation, there is, for us, now, an irony that is already a critique; some Pop artists have used this rather sophisticated device. What is important is that every time a "graphy," a school, has begun to stabilize, every time artists have begun reproducing a manner, an immediate attempt was made to find something else. There is, in modern art, a presence of desire, or rather, a presence in desire of the death drive—the presence of that which, in desire, generates movement. The sense of desire is composite: there is in desire what moves, what allows something else to appear, and on account of which it is always the same thing that returns. Desire is caught in phantasy; being caught in something, it is compulsive, but it also has the force to make this phantasizing turn, and this force makes desire wander over different objects. This is the function, a profoundly revolutionary function, that anti-art ought to perform. One could just as well take the American abstract expressionists of the period before Pop Art as an example, to show that, in a completely different field, without seeking objects in reality but by working at the level of the plastic screen itself, they produce, after all, a critique no less radical: it is obvious that in relation to Cubism (for they are the heirs of Cubism rather than Surrealism, even if a direct filiation exists with the latter), they go still a little further, realizing that even the cubist space is still a space of depth—it is deconstructed in comparison with Cartesian givens, but it remains a deep space; they reduce this deep space, which is still in some respects illusory because it is a screen within which desire can be lured, to a strictly two-dimensional space upon which expanses of color will be painted. On another properly optical level, there is an attempt to deconstruct a certain type of space inscription. I do not believe the function of art is to keep desire aroused in order that it *become* revolutionary, it *is* immediately revolutionary. At the present time, all plastic or musical expression either maintains the ilusion of a "formal" participation between people, or else attacks the deception of false communion.

III

Phantasy is obviously the primary issue. What links it with the problems previously considered is the question of power. Phantasy exists because desire bears within itself its prohibition, because—in Freudian terms still—desire can only be fulfilled in a regressive manner, through the formation of phantasies. This is the immediate meaning of the term. It is clear that phantasy is a direct derivative of prohibition, that is to say of the deepest form of power, naturally consubstantial with the unconscious. Phantasy cannot be freed for it contains within itself its prohibition; it is a *mise-en-scène* arising from desire's interdiction. The problem we should consider is that of the relation between art and these phantasy-formations. If the artist is someone who *expresses* his phantasies, if the relation is one of expression, the work only interests him or people who have complementary phantasies and who are thus able to fall in with it. Such an art will necessarily be repetitive: this is the case with Giacometti. I believe that the true art-phantasy relation is not direct; the artist does not externalize systems of internal figures, he is someone who undertakes to free *from* phantasy, *from* the matrix of figures whose heir and whose locus he is, what really belongs to the primary process, and is not a repetition, not a "graphy." Take the case of Klee; the first engravings are in the grip of phantasy, the plastic screen is treated as a window. They *represent* a woman in a tree, a woman followed by a weasel. Klee says so himself in his *Diaries*: I can draw at night, without *seeing* anything, this is the big difference with color. He speaks of his "inner stroke" as of something under the sway of phantasy. Direct expression is what he refers to here. But he is trying to depart from the always identical manner in which he approaches the sheet of paper. There are astonishing comments on this subject in the *Diaries*. Klee says, for example, that three things must be done: first, draw from nature, second, turn the page around and stress the important plastic elements, third, put the page back into the first position and attempt to reconcile the results of the first two operations. What is altogether remarkable is that Klee is thus perfectly describing the real relation of the artist with his phantasies, i.e. the double reversal. What he is attempting to do when things are upside down, is to free himself from the object, to keep desire's *mise-en-scène* from seducing him, to see the form itself, the stroke, the value, etc... By turning his drawing around, he reverses the relation between the represented and the formal system, he is *working*, and if he reverses representation, it is in order not to see the figurative, not to be the victim of phantasy any longer, in order to be able to work upon the plastic screen itself, upon the page, by producing strokes that have a certain formal relation between themselves. The two operations must subsequently be reconciled by reversing the sheet of paper once again. There is a reconciling function much like what Freud calls secondary elaboration. When this is resorted to, you have a work that is no longer jammed by phantasy, that is no longer blocked in a repetitive configuration, but on the contrary one that opens upon other possibilities, that *plays*, that sets itself up in the "inner-world": this is not the world of personal phantasy (and neither, obviously, is it that of reality); this is an *oscillating* work, in which there is room for the play of forms, a field liberated by the reversal of phantasy, but which still rests upon it. This has nothing to do with aesthetics and it does not necessarily produce hermetic works. Take the example of a widely distributed film: *Je t'aime, je t'aime*. A film of fiction. The subject: a man, who attempted suicide, is taken in hand by a group of scientists who think they can make man go back into the past. The film was very well received. What is truly astonishing is the articulation of the flash-backs. A real deconstruction of normal editing, which respects the spatio-temporal frameworks that are those of the secondary process, of reality-testing, is operated. What one is dealing with here is a total deconstruction of sequence. The subject finds himself in different time periods, and even the recurrence of the same scene from the past serves to deconstruct it. By inserting the whole thing in a very connoted science fiction context, Resnais succeeds in making it acceptable to a public, that, in general, goes to the cinema to "forget," in effect to find itself again, that is to say, not to look at the pictures, but to fulfill its own desires through them. I believe that Resnais obliges the public to stop phantasizing. The spectator finds himself in the reversing, critical, function of the work and his desire collides with the screen, because the screen is treated as a screen and not as a window. In the case of this film, the critical reversal is brought about by its cutting and editing. The work is the most difficult to do as far as the cinema, mass medium par excellence, is concerned. The cinema belongs to "culture," and three-fourths of its function consists in stirring up and in recovering phantasy by having it find fulfillment through the screen, by putting people in a situation of day-dreaming. The cinema—place of contact with the proletariat—is where certain things can be done: turning the spectator's attention around by reversing the space of representation and obliging him to unfulfill his desire is a revolutionary function.

What is there in phantasy? Is it a letter or a figure? For Klee, it is obviously a figure, for it is considered as a visible scene and not as a stage director. Even if phantasy is taken as a scenario, that is to say as a matricial configuration in the sense that Freud gives it in *A Child is Being Beaten*, two components, which Freud says are always united but which may in principle be separated, must be dissociated. And art actually consists in dissociating them for an instant: on the one hand, there is a repetitive element of *return*, for from the moment that desire is caught in phantasy, it is always "saying" the same thing; on the other hand, there is a dynamic which creates events to the extent that phantasy is very closely bound to the seeking of intense pleasure, itself the seeking of a difference between energetics brought to a maximum of tension and a complete discharge, the limit of this difference being death. This economy (in the Freudian sense) does not go in the direction of repetition, but in that of a constant seeking of the most intense difference. It is therefore a potential element of play in relation to repetition and writing. When Klee is at his best, he avoids reading phantasy as something that is always repeated; he allows himself to see, through the phantasy's graphy, elements—traces, values, colors—that play outside what is recognizable. A fundamental difference with the experience of Freud's magic writing pad should be noted. Klee says: the trace is there, I am keeping it and turning it around, I continue to work with the same trace operating upon its displacements, condensations, etc. What he is concerned with is thus the primary process, but from the point of view of its form.

The poet who does no more than "express himself" is completely bound by his phantasy, and being always bound by the same elements, he is not a poet. He produces a falsely figural text, the figural traces of which are but those of his phantasies. A certain kind of syntactical construction will be seen to reappear, one will eventually be able to speak of his "style," there will be a semantics and syntax that are the spontaneous legacy of his phantasy. These are the elements Mauron takes into consideration in order to analyse Mallarmé's poems. The method he adopts rests, however, on a serious misconception, because the assumption is that Mallarmé remains wholly prisoner of his phantasies, whereas what is interesting is to see how, out of this, Mallarmé endeavors to deconstruct the graphy of his phantasy. These deconstructions obviously remain figures. I do not mean that the subject becomes aware of his phantasies and that everything makes its way to consciousness, to the ego. What is quite astonishing is the formal level, is that the deconstruction operates, with the energetics proper to the primary process, upon that which in the phantasy, does not truly belong to the primary process: it operates upon what is already a graphy produced by repression.

IV

We must not continue, according to an old political tradition, to subordinate art directly to a political function. To allow thus that the function of arousing, of exasperating desire that is performed by the work of art, ought to have as its end the instigation of revolutionary motivations in those to whom it is presented, so that this work of exasperating desire has its end not in itself, but in the other thing, in a political attitude, would mean, in effect, that art has an ideological function. But this will have to be thought through: strictly speaking, this means that art has a delusionary function, that this arousal of desire is in fact something that functions as a screen for something else. Works of art will be presented, that, in effect, are going to exasperate desire in people, but precisely in order to bring about an attitude geared to practical transformation in the Marxist sense, to the transformation of the reality of social relations, and on an even deeper level, of the relations of production. Thus, the work of art is only there as a means to an end, and its properly aesthetic operations, particularly in the case of painting, have no revolutionary value in and of themselves, but indirectly, through their end. This is unacceptable; no illusion is ever revolutionary. If desire can be fulfilled in the work of art, then the work of art gives something to hope for. I believe that what is revolutionary is precisely to hope for nothing. Critique's extraordinary force in the work of art, inasmuch as one is dealing with presences—plastic or musical— springs from the fact that one is always in the order of the here- now; it is here and now that the critical reversal operates. To hang the meaning of the work of art upon its subsequent political effect is once again not to take it seriously, to take it for an instrument, useful for something else, to take it as a *representation* of something to come; this is to remain within the order of representation, within a theological or teleological perspective. This is to place the work of art, even when one is dealing with non or anti-representational works, within a (social, political) space of representation. This leaves politics as representation uncriticized.

In traditional Marxism, the problem of constituting a political consciousness is the problem of constituting a discourse capable of signifying reality as it can be experienced, that is to say of transcribing reality into a coherent discourse by saying that, at the level of the factory, for example, if there is a work speed-up, it is, first, because the foreman and the time-keeper told the boss a speed-up was possible, insofar as they believe the workers will tolerate it, but, more importantly still, because surplus-value is going to increase, as will the boss's profits and his business competitiveness on a national or a world-wide scale, and because such is the system's end: to reproduce capital by expanding it. Such a discourse can be coherently developed; he who utters it is assumed to have a political consciousness and, by the same token, to be capable—if he is not a schizophrenic—of transforming the reality he is talking about. In other words, we do find Freud's two criteria again: verbalization and the possible transformation of things. What struck me in May 1968 was this: something happened precisely to the extent that this type of discourse, if it kept on being produced, at least had absolutely no relation whatsoever with the real unsettling of things; it even had an inverse relation to it. The people who believed in their own political awareness continued to hold this kind of discourse, and it was easy to see that their utterances, very far from promoting the real transformation of things, helped to keep them as they stood. The true problem, politically as well as from an "artistic" point of view (and only anti-art is possible), is the inverse. The system, as it exists, absorbs every consistent discourse; the important thing is not to produce a consistent discourse but rather to produce "figures" within reality. The problem is to endure the anguish of maintaining reality in a state of suspicion through direct practices; just like, for example, a poet is a man in a position to hold language—even if he uses it—under suspicion, i.e. to bring about figures which would never have been produced, that language might not tolerate, and which may never be audible, perceptible, for us.

Political people take refuge behind this conviction: the proletariat, in any case, will "succeed" because it is in a good position to do so, and, besides it, there are a few petty bourgeois, students, etc., who, dragging in tow, must pass through a formal revolt in order to reach revolutionary consciousness. Let us look at what is happening without prejudice. Let us not believe that the proletariat will encounter art later on. This encounter is in reality the immediate question before politics. If the proletariat does not grasp the fact that the question now is one of a deconstruction, here and now, of the economic and social forms within which it is caught, if it does not see a direct relation between anti-art or pop art's deconstruction and what must be done *against* the politics of politicians, if it does not perceive that there is something absolutely analogous between what must be done today to social reality and what is done on a canvas or within a sonorous space, not only will it not encounter the problem of art, it will never come upon revolution. Those who hold a consistent discourse on behalf of the proletariat will continue to speak in its name, and to say what it wants, in its place. They will say for example that universities must be constructed in a realist-socialist style.

V

Avant-garde means that artists show the way. To whom? Historically the concept was firt political, Leninist: the party shows the way to the social class. The model is a military model borrowed from the practices of eighteenth-and-nineteenth-century armies. It has lost all relevance in its field of origin, and has no metaphoric relevance in political matters. It has never had any relevance whatsoever as far as art goes; it was simply the result of a reassuring but unthinkable transfer: expressive power should be won under the same conditions as strategic (or political) power. What is in question is the fulfilling of desire, of an ideology. There can be no contact between the proletariat and the "avant-garde," this, paradoxically, because they both arise out of the same crisis: "art" does not exist for the proletariat because capitalism has made it a separate activity, has completed the destruction of the old "religious" forms of communication; and it is for the same reason that artists want none of this solitary passtime, and that some of them find consolation in thinking of themselves as an avant-garde ("avant-garde" is an antidotal word coined by the spirit of capitalism that enables it to recuperate any isolation). What exists in the way of expression for the proletariat are the mass media, subway posters, advertising at the movies, pop music, T.V. variety shows. These are the forms it has access to, with this two-fold specificity: the amateur's activity is placed in the passive, and the form is directly subordinated to the interests of capital. These are the forms through which desire is fulfilled and, consequently, lost, which also means that the proposed forms, whatever their nature, may never be taken seriously since they are only there to fulfill desire which, in fulfilling itself, reduces them to nothing. Desire does not take the image seriously, it needs images, but in order to be able to kill them. This is the possible point of encounter, the object of the protocol of collaboration between the capitalist system and the economy of desire: not to take forms seriously, but only as a detour, as a moment leading back to something other tham themselves (to the so-called "reality" of capitalism, to the pseudo "satisfaction" of needs). I believe this is the only observable relation between the proletariat and "art." The problem is badly posed, however, for this relation is not a relation. In fact, what is interesting is the proletariat's relation with art, not as a separate field (because precisely what I do hope is that, in a socialist society, there will be no "art," we must have a society in which there will no longer be painters, but people who paint), but with anti-art. What happened in France in May '68, and what is now taking place elsewhere, is the discontinuous formation—the bursting forth, then the vanishing—of situations that are situations of deconstruction, that disconcert discourse and social reality. It is on this very level that junctions can occur between students and workers, on this level of an absolutely practical art which consists, precisely, in deconstructing not the material, plastic screen of representation—not an automobile as in the case of pop artists—but the ideological screen of representation, a subway station as a social space, for example, people's relation to the public transport system taking them to work, their relation to subway tickets, their relation with one another, or with the hierarchical organisation of a workshop, a factory, or a university, etc. This has a direct connection with art, not with the avant-garde, but with anti-art, with that capacity to seek out and to maintain forms that are neither realist forms at the level of perception, not signifiable within an articulated discourse. It must also be recognized, however, that such forms can appear, completely disconcert the institution, rock it in a formidable fashion and then perhaps disappear; this fluidity ought to be related to what Freud describes as the artist's capacity to let forms appear that issue from the unconscious and penetrate into the secondary process, that is to say into realist and conscious practice. Such forms can only be ephemeral traces. These, much more than a greater political consciousness, are the terms of the current revolutionary problem, which should be posed rather in terms of a *letting go* of consciousness.

VI

If you look at one of the most effective works of pop art, it exactly satisfies the conditions of sexual climax, i.e. an extreme tension with a profound release. It is a plastic space, organized in a certain way, in which one element destroys the whole organization. This corresponds to the definition that, after Freud, orgasm must be given: the collaboration of Eros and death, the seeking of the most complex, the most differentiated organization, and its destruction. Things like this could be seen at the level of social reality, no longer in museums, but in the streets. For example, the first time a street barricade was put up: an unlikelihood that completely disconcerts urban space—a space devised so that people may circulate within it; suddenly this space rises up, figures crop up that have no relation whatsoever to the traffic, no strategic function at all. As we know, the barricades were deplorable in this respect, they have no hold at all on reality, but are traces of another process. The effect of anxiety, of disconcertion was prodigious for everyone. One was then dealing with true anti-art. The second time, desire repeats, finds, recognizes itself, is recovered by the second barricade. This means that the critical function is a function that ought to work without pause. The idea that the revolutionary society is a society that *will have* its institutions is an absurd one. It will be a society wherein what Freud calls suspended attention will be practiced, wherein figures will not cease appearing, and will have to be put up with. It will be the society pervaded with the maximum of anxiety. If it be said now that the barricades had no lasting effect whatsoever at the level of the secondary process, at the "political" level, the answer is easy: one negative thing is certain, twenty or ten years of secondary discourse, of a supposedly concerted effectiveness had changed nothing, one night of primary process changed many things. Today everyone knows that the ground of the system can overturn. But it is absolutely certain that there is no guarantee. This is an anti-politics. A certain kind of discourse, a certain kind of organization or effectiveness are things dead. The class struggle appears when there are direct actions, critical-practical actions, as Marx used to say: it is at this moment that the lower middle-class's relation to art is completely stripped of its ideological elements because it becomes perceptible that art itself as a separate existence is a mystification and presents no interest whatsoever; it is also at this moment that the proletariat has an immediate and practical access to the truth of art, i.e. to the (direct and non-subordinated) deconstruction of social forms. The position of political people is that, on the one hand, there is art, and on the other, politics, and that this politics, which is supposedly the proletariat's, ought to appropriate art and put it into its service. The problem they raise thus is a false problem, they forget to ask themselves if there is an art. Well, these precious "artists" do ask themselves where and how it exists. They, as a matter of fact, no longer want to paint for museums. So they are asked to paint for factories, but they see no difference. And they are right: factory and museum are tail and head of a same coin. The coin has to be changed, not the side of the coin. An "artist" is someone who presents problems of forms. The essential element, the only decisive one, is form. Modifying social reality is not important at all if it aims at putting back into place something that will have the *same form*. What is important, above all, is to cease sympathizing with artists, what must be understood is the true problem they are putting before political people. There is more revolution, even if it is not much, in American Pop art that in the discourse of the Communist party.

Translated by Susan Hanson

Gift of Organs

There are plastic invariables, chromatic or graphic elements, or values, which Kandinsky, Klee, Itten, Albers sought to define, few in number. But their value does not lie in their opposition one to another within a system; they have value by themselves, by a certain modality of postural or motorial resonance they arouse in the body. They are not arbitrary. Their perceptible presence is all their immediate value: if they were to be perceived in isolation, as in those observations made of victims of cerebral palsy, where the patient is placed in a room lit entirely in red or green, or as in the large monochromatic canvases of Op art, they would not lose any of their absolute force. Blue, in principle, organizes a space of withdrawal, of "adduction" or organic silence; the broken line makes its surroundings quiver; the pale comes forward from the dark. To all these movements, our body lends itself, built on the same code, transcribing value from one field to another. Certainly, you can combine, set off, or neutralize this color with another one; which proves that no syntax, no "graphy," forces plastic elements to be connected according to infrangible constraints.

The plastic object is not a message, it is not a vehicle of communication chartered for the best possible transport of information. The more plastic it is, the fewer informative elements it contains. The painter, the sketcher, do not talk to us through their lines and colors. The thing they make is meant to be given. The child also gives his shit to what he loves.

A line is not for hearing, for understanding, is not a letter. The letter is a line alienated from the space where it is inscribed, just as signification transcends the perceptible. The letter is not directed to the body; the line, however, exists only through the echo that it will encounter in the bodies where it will generate itself as danceable volume, polyphony, scene, texture at palpitating fingertips. It will suspend speech. It will be the other side of words, the order of silence, of the scream, hushing all emitters and receivers. It imposes the other of discourse, it is movement in its simplicity erecting sense.

What is this reception given by the hand that traces it, the eye that roves over it? What is active, what passive? Why give lines, figures?

Turn the question around. One does not *give* pieces of information. For either you are not aware of those concealed in your discourse, and you do not give them, they slip by with it, gathered or not by your interlocutor; or else you think you know them (and allow me to doubt it), and you use their transmission for business or power, and not at all as a gift. The gift of discourse is well short of/beyond these positions of circuit control, the positions of a mediator alienated from what he mediates, as Marx used to say, positions of the passions for domination and possession. When discourse becomes gift, it gives almost no information, the text or speech in its turn becomes a thing rather than a message, figure inhabits it like a siren's song; receive it and give thanks, it is not meant to be understood.

One gives a representation. One gives when speech is lacking, one gives things, not messages, even if these things are made of words. The figure is what gives (itself). It is not the text that is given, but the representation that dwells in it. Every gift is figural. I see the Sphinx lying over Oedipus, scrutinizing the delirium of he who thinks to use words to help decipher enigmas and who speaks even under her claws, just when she is readying to let him go and thus to destroy him, to condemn him to fulfilling his destiny. I see her face, with its willowlike flowing auburn tresses, spellbind the innocent countenance, slightly flushed, of the prince of speech, the pitiless and rectilinear crest of her nostrils, the closed ear lobes and the matt cylinder of the nape of her neck, and I clearly see that what ruins Oedipus, and us after him, is being unable to receive the figure when it offers itself.

Nonetheless, from the imperturbable astonishment of the

chestnut eyes, the icy heat of the chest crushing his chest, the smooth shoulder looming over him, he must have felt in a flash the premonition that the female monster that had knocked him down in order to tear him apart was truth at the same time as death. And he must have hesitated a second, wondering if it would not be better to let himself be seduced by death and truth than to have an answer to everything. But Oedipus is not Orpheus.

We cannot receive the figure, we are not even capable of letting it make its path and its trace on our eye. Figure that cannot be looked at, always already repressed because it is that of desire. The intelligible message takes the place of the Egyptian stare; and it dissipates it, and thus the speaker, the philosopher, feels reassured: he has defeated the figural with his words. He is unaware, however, that succubus' soft (but cutting) chestnut pupil, which he is relieved not to see fixed upon him any more has become the pupil of his own discourse: the figure has passed into his own speech, and while he thinks he is making reason with his mouth, his words are full of eyes, his clarities full of night.

There is a primal terror: each one of us, on his own account, has been seized by something absent; in the area opened by lack, desire has unfolded its figures. Will we be mad enough to say that the figure deceives us? But it is in the place of . . . *nothing*. What deceives is to put some signified in this place. The depth of the Egyptian eyes is perhaps an empty depth: this emptiness is nonetheless more faithful to the primary absence where the figure-making vertigo unrolled its spirals than the peaceful Odyssey of discourse. By withdrawing from us, by ceasing to answer us, a voice has defied all voices, it has plunged us into the misery of interminable explanations, of security-seeking, of excuse-making, of confessions of finitude. Try rather to stare at the figure born of silence and to re-present it, that is, give it. Which is what this poet, this sketcher, do.

Who do they give their figures to? To this absence. They leave its place vacant, they do not make questions and answers, they know well that there is no dialogue, that the violence of a law has interrupted the promised response, they take upon themselves the deficiency of words, the interruption of communication; like musicians now, they make sense with *fading*.

But these are the beginnings of art, still supplication, spell-casting. Like the phallus freshly withdrawn from the vagina, the figure vibrates and shines with anxiety, even though put on stage and exhibited. It is outside, it is still within. Now it is remarkable that the phantasy's immanence to the work determines its degree of *graphy*, of plastic rigidity, that the more the literary or pictorial form emanates from the deep matrix where desire is caught, the more there emerges from the series of writings or drawings, by repetition, a sort of language of signs, a singular discourse that the phantasy "speaks" and which holds the work under its claw. Here we are plunged into necessity, emerging little. Hence the grip of the scream. . .

We don't have yet the second Yea, by which the phantasm's grip will unclench and thanks to which any signified whatsoever, any throw of the dice will be able to be played on the stage of representation. The second Yea may bring about the real dance; The Sphinx represented; this is the initial scream, when you look at the figure straight on for the first time at the risk of becoming speechless and when you have to hold up under the gust of blood-chill that this inspection earns you. One cannot say Yea, one cannot already be capable of speaking about something else, while speaking of this, thanks to the play, to the dance of metaphors, of displacements; you are always trying to speak of this figure to keep it in check, to protect, between the long eyes of Egypt and your tongue, the narrow space which immediate breath needs in order to renew itself. Afterwards, you will see, the eye will open up, the figural space reinvested by the space of representation will perhaps permit the dance.

These drawings are the brethren of the texts in the pressure of anxiety. . .

This fascination which makes the "series," is that which the encounter with the deep figures causes. Indecipherable, withdrawn into its night, it stalks the pencil, pushes it to form the same stroke again and again, it makes itself the author of the author, and what it traces is the unalterable emblem of its absence. Imagine Oedipus, lying under the Sphinx still, having renounced words, having renounced "wanting to get out" (of this sorry predicament!), drawing with a steel hand what he sees in the monster's eyes: A close-up of his own fear, his own icy hand, his genitals crushed.

Why these organs cut out and given on the stage of the text or drawing? Why is the first, the only possible gift, when the figure is still so close, that of the fragmented body? Because the fear of the knife in the figure's soft eye. . . ?

To be seduced is to be separated from oneself, led outside oneself. Every seduction is disjunction, tearing of the friable image of itself that the ego tries to construct. We have our unity in the primitive figure that looks at us, and that unity is outside us; we can only catch a glimpse of it at the price of cutting up the place of life, of making a gift of organs. This price of death is that of the offering owed the Sphinx. Whoever doesn't pay it will be led astray in and by his reasons. To be deconstructed, torn apart, is the lot of he who wants to see truth. Nothing guarantees that he will gain a work from this excruciation.

It is probable that the work as well must first be lost. Like all that presents itself in conciliation, as reconciliation. The sacrifice of organs does not appease the knife-eye of the knowing virgin. She will never be our concubine but always our mistress. There is no longer any religion to tie the organs back together, today the gift of offal stays here, on these plates, in these words, we know that there is no one left to raise it toward the Other and remit our anguish. The work is still a priestly notion, it belongs to the device of dialectic. This fragmentation is not a moment, it cannot be sublated, at the most it is playable, re-presentable. These hard broken figures strewing these words and these drawings are the figures of gaiety.

Translated by Richard Lockwood

Several Silences

Desire thought in terms of a lack, of negativity; and desire produced in words, sounds, colors, volumes in terms of the idea of the positive processes. Desire *of* something, desire period. Desire that fashions, in the void, the double (the phantasy, the copy, the *replica*, the hologram) *of* what it lacks, desire as work, aimless metamorphosis, play without memory. The two acceptations are, in Freud: *Wunsch*, the primary processes. The affirmative properties identified in the latter shelter them from all "thought," from a partitioning that would section their energetics into articuli and set intervals. The positivity of the Id is why the Ego shall never be where it was, why their reconciliation is a factual impossibility, and why they cannot form a unity (that of a subject, of a work— even an "open" work, of a society, of a body). By introducing the idea of the death drive, Freud means to *reinforce* the economy and the affirmative nature of the primary processes (thereby displacing both). The death drive is simply the fact that energy does not have an ear for unity, for the concert of the organism (of the "psychic apparatus"); it is deaf to the organism's composition, i.e. to the lack, the void in which the organs, the articuli (the notes) would be carved out and arranged to make a cosmos and a *musike*. Eros composes music. The death drive is never heard, it is silent, says Freud. This because it is libidinal economy's deafness to the rules of composition, to the hierarchy of the organism.

Neither the Commune nor May 1968 were heard coming, sounding notes of preparation. Inversely, both kept on hearing all too well the sweet music of the social organism. To see badly, says Nietzsche, is to see too little; to hear badly, is to hear too much. Too many harmonics.

The death drive is not just another drive; it is randomness. Freud approaches it through suffering: nightmares of traumatised neúrotics, failure syndromes or fate compulsions, repetitions of the loss of an object. But, he adds, in orgasm itself, at the heart of Eros and composition, so they say, there is still drifting, excess, annihilation of the regulated. Extreme sufferings, extreme joys; excessive tensions, deep depressions. Composition stays within the norms of intensity, within average intensities, under regulation. The death drive is marked by surges of tension, what Klossowski calls *intensities*, Cage *events*. Dissonances, stridences, positively exaggerated, ugly, silences.

The secondary process is a binding process. A sound is a noise that is bound, related to an articulation of the sound continuum (the scale), to a production set-up (stringed-instrument factory), to a syntax (counterpoint), to a rhetoric (the sonata form). In the final instance, a sound, insofar as it is bound, has value not for its sonority but for the network of its actual and possible relations, just like the phoneme, a distinctive arbitrary unit. (Adorno emphasizes that all unified works of art are pseudomorphoses of verbal language and that from the very start organic music, a descendant of the *recitativo* style, imitates speech. He also stresses that dodecaphonic music establishes itself as protest by eliminating unification—but that is not enough.) Composition is a desensitization of material. (It reaches its limit with Schönberg, says Adorno.) Desensitization, this introduces a reference to the body. But which one? What is hearing? A phenomenological schema of the body functions implicitly in Adorno, but *also in Cage*: uncompleted unity of sense, always in the process of constituting itself along with and at the same time as the world; but unity just the same, and of sense. Or if you prefer: sound world bringing itself about in the unity of a body. Or still, perceptual ante-predicating *cogito*. Thus, sense, cogito, the conscious. Phenomenology situates the body as a region where *the* sounds transform themselves into music, where the unbound (un-conscious) is bound, where noise becomes sonority. (There is very little on music in the *Phenomenology of Perception*, more in the *Phenomenology of Aesthetic Experience*: but for Merleau-Ponty, as for Dufrenne, music is in the method: abundance of metaphors on rhythm, consonance, being in tune, resonating force, synesthesia, constant assault on neo-Kantianism as music from the head.) The phenomenological body is a body that composes, a body possessed with Eros. But to compose is always to filter out and to bind, to exclude entire regions of the sound world as noise and to produce "music" (that which is "audible") with the input. The noises rejected by the body, be it a body that composes, are not heard. If they are, it is as dissonances, as flows of sound entering a device not prepared to receive them and transform them into music. The phenomenological body is a filter and requires, then, that whole sound regions be desensitized.

Inversely, the sensitization to the material will be extreme, requiring the virtual destruction of the filtering device (stimuli shield, says Freud); it will be intensive potency, potency of the intensities, and will not refer to the unity of the musician-musical body but to surges in tension, to intense singularities. In fact, there is no device to receive these intensities: their singularity consists in their not being related by memory to units of reference (a scale, rules of harmony, or their hypothetical equivalent in the phenomenological body); there is no region in which to measure them. It is not enough to say, as Cage says his father said: *Measurement, he said, measure measuring means*, which is phenomenological, i.e., erotico-logical, body that constitutes itself while constituting the world and music. What should be said is that no unity, no comprehensive unity, no composition is made with *this* noise, *this* sound, *this* singular intensity, but rather *in spite of* them. To hear this event is to transform it: into tears, gestures, laughter, dance, words, sounds, theorems, repainting your room, helping a friend move. I can testify to the fact that a black cat (Lhermite) heard Kagel's *Music for Renaissance Instruments*: bristling of whiskers, fluttering of ears, prowling in the vicinity of the listening room. The intensity of noise-sound = an urge to produce something, circumstantially, in an endless return where nothing repeats itself. What is needed to make these metamorphoses possible is the indisposition of the composer-body (the phenosocial body) rather than the gray metaphors of the discomposer in the musical museum. *He was a physicist and a computer-composer in his spare time. Why was he so stupid? Because he was of the opinion* (asks Cage) *that the only thing that will engage the intellect is the measurement of the relations between things?*

What is called music is a device:

1—that invests libido mainly in the sound region: a commutator of libidinal energy into audible energy and vice versa; which implies to start with that quantities of energy are constantly used to circumscribe this region, on the body particularly (e.g., to disconnect the phonatory and auditory cavities from the motor organs: dancing);

2—that in classical and baroque periods in the West, has appended musical prostheses, instruments, to this partial body; an adjunction which required new investments onto certain parts of the body: the hands, the fingers of the pianist or the flutist, but also the arm-shoulder-chin complex of the violinist, the torso of the percussionist, the knees of the cellist and harpist;

3—that produces only discontinuous sounds whose pitches can be located to the nearest half-tone in a fixed division of sound-space;

4—that favors the key of C and treats five out of twelve half-tones as subordinate, "transitional" notes;

5—that, in the name of tonality, tolerates only that distribution of intervals between pitches given by the "Pythagorean" mode;

6—that privileges, in the name of chords, aggregates of three degrees separated respectively by intervals of a third;

7—that in the key of C, gives preeminence to major chords called perfect, placed on the first, fourth, and fifth degrees;

8—etc., I hand this matter over to those more knowledgeable than myself, it isn't difficult.

The purpose of this list is to show what a device is, i.e. a superimposition of grids that filter flows of energy, in this case, sound. These grids are not things (there are no things): they are libidinal investments that block the entrance and exit of certain sound-noises, and that maintain and transmit themselves. A major portion of the libidinal potential is used in these policed-policing functions. Horror should the device produce a sound noise excluded on principle: listening to a singer, as a child, I was, I still am terrified and curious of two possibilities: she will forget the words (F!), she will start to sneeze. When Tudor and Cage gave *Mureau+Rainforest* in Basel, a group of protesters near Andrée and myself started to shout, to imitate mooings, whinnyings: no uproar, their doings fit right into the performance. They should have broadcast a Bach Suite at ear-splitting volume, and even then. . .

The dissonances in baroque classical music are "prepared" and then "resolved." A light tension is created by a tiny dissonance, and it is washed away with a tonic chord. The dominant seventh chord, writes Barraud, "contains a certain interval that creates an irresistible pull (. . .) It wants to be resolved in a perfect cadence on a tonic chord." (But, adds Barraud in parentheses, "an irresistible pull that modern musicians resist quite well, however.") "A tension-producing apparatus," says the same author regarding dissonance, "that multiplies the dynamism (of the tonal system) and brings out the tonal function." What is this play of dynamization against a background of reinforced identity? Dysfunction creates a desire to restore good form. This is the *fort/da* game. It is the transmutation of libido as energy into desire as *Wunsch*. The positive *drifting* of the former becomes the negativity of the latter, its mimed lack-of-object. "From Monteverdi to Verdi," writes Adorno, "dramatic music, as true *musica ficta*, presented expression in the form of stylized mediated expression, i.e. as the appearance of passions." The pair dissonance-resolution is a good introduction to the question of *appearance* in music: because it is constitutive of *depth*. This touches on the libidinal mainspring of *theatricality*, on the profound congruency of musical and theatrical spectacle in the West of the "classical" period, on the preeminence of opera, on the conditions that made the invention of cinema possible. Not to mention politics.

The pair *fort-da* is not the sequence *da-fort*; *da-fort* is a dissonance, *fort-da* is its resolution. The repetition of *fort!* is dependent upon the repetition of *da!*. The intensity of all suffering (anxiety) is brought down to the simple fear of losing, and to the regret of having lost, an object. Domination of Eros, which envelops and disfigures drifting in play-activity. This domination produces the mise-en-scène: the edge of the bed is the frame of the stage, entrances and exits of the wooden spool, *Sprechgesang* of the child in the wings. This is the Cave.

Politics is not only the void, negativity, the chiasma of sociality by which the latter accomplishes itself (phenomenology of politics); politics is also what spreads over and effaces these elements, the *production of appearance*, tying up the unraveled into a theatrical set-up analogous to *fort-da*. The primary processes are overlooked, they are mimed in a spectacle-like negativity: "You are unhappy because an object—wooden spool, property, work, freedom, pleasure—was snatched from you." The dissonance is prepared: it is only substraction. And so it will be resolved by totalization.

The privilege granted tonic, dominant, and sub-dominant chords, is the prevalence of the whole over the parts; these three chords, together, give *all* the degrees of the scale. Resolution indicates totality. Dialectics and dialectical politics are also based on the principle that if you "have" organic totality, then dissonances (conflicts, struggles, disorder, injustices, inequalities) disappear. Dissonance is alienation, part taken for the whole; dissonance resolves itself in the *good* viewpoint, that of the whole, that of the composer, who is the Prince of Sounds, the Secretary of their Party.

If I were a knowledgeable musicologist, I would venture to write this: the *effect of depth* (constitutive of theatricality) can be elucidated by examining the hierarchy of sounds in classical music. It should be noted, for instance, that a dissonance can be resolved into a tonic chord only because the ear of memory, when it hears the dissonant chord or the dominant chord, anticipates the path to be followed across sound space so as to reach the goal.

"Depth" implies that one is both here and there at the same time: here, in the dissonance, the ear already hears the perfect chord there. And if it can be there already, it is because it knows the path that leads there (cadence). So it is that time is "dominated." In painting, *costruzione legittima* fills the same function for space: with orthogonals, the mind's eye travels over the distance that separates the foreground from the background while it constructs it. The background *resolves* the foreground. *Costruzione legittima* not only "penetrates the support" by masking its bi-dimensionality but also obliterates the whole peripheral zone in visual space: curved, anamorphic, turbulent, accidental. The tonal system also disguises the time-surface, the time of events: the tonic chord is suspended throughout a multiplicity of themes and variations, therefore it neutralizes them as appearances to be resolved, just as the diversity of the visual datum is resolved in the system of orthogonals that leads the eye to the commanding point. Appearance arises from this set-up. Depth (and thus appearance) comes into existence only as resolution, reconciliation, or totalization of multiplicity in the unity of the vanishing point or the tonic, secondarisation. If I were a logical musicologist, I would venture to add this: analogous in its effect is the rise to power of harmony over melody in baroque music. In plainchant, wholly separate voices wander, meet, come apart, paths indifferent to chords and subsequently privileged bass lines. In romantic music, this multiplicity is brought together under the laws of harmony by the science of counterpoint. Melody operates not for itself, then, but as an appearance; surface effect referring to a background by means of harmonic construction. Same device for mise-en-scène, with the director's silence, with the traces of work effaced.

To construct surfaces as appearance is to *construct*: to produce actions that will be taken as the effects of something else, of an Other, not as event, not as what happens. The secret of building, of *fabbrica*: plane, elevation. The stage is a building, architecture becomes a stage production. Brunelleschi, Francesco di Giorgio, Palladio. It is not that architectural construction precedes other constructions; the same function is everywhere: to produce surfaces as appearances, as *skènai*, scoenae, curtain-screens. Including the surface of volumes, as attested by the set-up of the Olympic Theater at Vicenza. Similarly, the *Konstruktion* in analysis, such as Freud describes it in later works, produces the discourse of the patient as symptom, surface.

To produce a surface as appearance is to produce surface as a site of inscription. But what if the Renaissance had not invented or re-invented appearance in painting, music, architecture, politics; what if general theatricalization had not come about? Then there would have been no surface as site of inscription; impossible even the category of inscription, which implies dissociation of an agent (director, painter, architect, composer, prince) and a patient (the would-be zone of inscription, wax, blank slate, the people [dialectically become the masses], the analysand [dialectically become the analyst]). One has to think the primary processes on the near side of generalized theatricalization and inscription, as connections and transformations of inflow and outflow, without ever being able to decode what is active or passive in the connection. Thus, without inscriptibility and without surface. Surfaces of inscription (canvas stretched in its frame, stage set, tonal framework, offices and chambers of political deliberation and decision), these surfaces are themselves flows of stabilized quiescent libidinal energy, functioning as locks, canals, regulators of desire, as its figure-producing figures. No goal, no cause, no reason: a formation of Eros that brings to a halt the nomadism of the death drive, that reduces the intensities.

When Leriche says that health is the silence of the organs, he shows that he does not have an ear, that he has the classic European policed-policing ear. In an anechoic chamber, Cage's body (which was feeling just fine) made noise; pulsations of the circulatory system, neural impulses. The silence of the bodily organs makes a tremendous racket. Try an earplug sometime. Death, certain illnesses are just as silent as health in the performance of their task. Contrary to Leriche, Freud states that the death drive is always silent, stiffled in the rumblings of Eros; and it is health that makes noise (musically, nevertheless). The pertinent alternatives are not: noise or silence. Silence as the ideal of health is the neurosis of that Europe which orders the following representation: to reduce drives to silence, to keep them on the outside (the *limes*, first surface), to disseminate the reassuring image of the unified body offering the solid armor of its bronzed stimuli shield to the exterior, with nothing, the void, left to hear "inside." This was already the sculpture-in-the-round and the well-oiled athletics of the Greeks.

But truth is elsewhere. The "surface" of the body is not comparable to a stage curtain or cinema screen or painter's canvas. It is full of holes, or rather, the holes are part of the skin; skin involutes by hollowing out the so-called "inside" (point of view of the theater), which is just as external as the "outside." The "good form" on the "inside" as silence, is the empty, purged body; it is the obliteration of the body as noise-sound to the benefit of an orchestra-conducting body, the operator musically effaced, annihilated. From the silence of noise, plural, to the silence of order. What prevails today is the silence of the prince, placed in the privileged seat in the theater of Serlio and Palladio, the silence demanded of the public in the concert hall, and of the stage machinery and stagehands. When his health is good, Leriche, the doctor, the prince, must not be able to hear the hypothetical director of the body, the stage pit, the wings, the upper flies, the innards, the pumps for blood, air, piss, shit, and sperm. Silence arising from an obliteration, thus, counterpart of appearance.

When Mao swims across the Yangtse Kiang, his body makes noise, the opposition between inside and outside crumbles. Could the Prince, then, no longer be the grand Mute situated for evermore at the right viewing distance, in his tribune on the square in Peking, watching the crowd, seeing his own image reflected by the crowd, hearing not the libido rumbling in the bodies, but a single voice reciting-singing mao-thought? Swimming the crawl in the bay, breathing right then left, consequently every one-and-a-half strokes, there are: (1) sounds propagated underwater, for example, the high-pitched sounds coming from very far away (boat propellers) along with their harmonics, the low-pitched sounds of bubbling left by kicking feet, especially the carillon of exhaled air bubbles that slide and burst along the ears; (2) alternately: a) when the ear out of the water is turned toward shore, all the rumblings in the city, the beach, with singular bursts of noise, a bell, fire sirens, a horn, a loudspeaker, the squeals of children taking a dip nearby, b) when the ear opens onto the open sea, the nearby lapping of waves that lick the ear, small masses of water rubbing against one another, farther away the purrings of a motor, the cries of seagulls. While doing the crawl, the body pivots, turns entirely on its longest axis, and this opens one ear while closing the other, alternately. The movement serves as a machine for producing sounds, a musical instrument, *but the noises produced by the movement itself belong to these sounds*. Feet beating like oar blades, arms scooping up like forks; beating, scooping—what? Things? no, energy, inertia, thus making friction and impact, deep inhalation and forceful exhalation, the heart joining its beat to this hubbub. One shouldn't say that the body cannot be heard in its exertion and this frolic (another of Leriche's ideas). The body is an operator of movable sound to be sure, but of its own sounds; its noisy workings are involved in this action. What is happening is not what is supposed to happen according to the ideology of "physical culture," body mastery, etc.; what is happening is movement and music without appearances. Not domination, but metamorphosis. Knowing how to do the crawl is not power-over, but sound (and touch, color) potencies. Swimming next to a friend, we don't want the power of one over the other or over the water, to show that one is stronger than the other, to beat the clock, etc., other obsessional and paranoid impulses that are nourished by the minds of politics and political economy, we don't want to beat anything, win anything, just make music together. When I breathe in his direction, one eye and one ear out of the water, I see his nose slide along as if set upon the water, I hear the slapping of his palms seeking the surface again and again. . . he swims as if he were flying (I, more like a ponderous cetacean), at times we are on the same rhythm, at times we fall out of step, and that alone is just as fine as the polyrhythmic invention of the *Rite of Spring*. Not mastery of the body, but dissolution into workings.

A description much too phenomenological still, unduly marked by the empirical subject. It should be shown that this device is made up of stases of energy: regulation of the respiratory rhythm, synchronization of the movements of hands and shoulders, desynchronization of the arms and legs, locking of the knees, suppleness of the ankles, etc., i.e. a series of investments that make possible this mode of dancing in water. Under this, the unforseeable, the mad arbitrariness of desire investing itself in the device and enabling you to do the crawl. And to be counted along with it, the rebellion of the primary processes, which suddenly undo the swimmer, make him choke, laugh, stop, panic, make the gears grind.

"Like a fish in water," should be expressed as: the dissolution of appearance, the suppression of the theatrical relation between the Prince—the potential prince in every militant—and the masses (= people who are well-positioned, who hear *too much*, who are immersed in noise, resonance, echoes, reverberations). In any case: not like the leader on the tribune. And not like the operative machine in its medium, either. Imagine water threatening to drown a fish. Or teaching it that a fish is made of water. Imagine a storm: the fine fish's music dissolved and covered over by the rustling of the undercurrents and the reverberations of the breakers.

In the middle of the night, way in the back of the apartment (= late nineteenth-century bourgeois apartment), he heard what all the adults around him called a "scene," "to make a scene," human noises but of inhuman intensity, pitch, duration. He got up *without a sound* = with the old bed groaning, the floor boards creaking, the door squeaking, he went closer to the imagined source, the door to the parents' room, the equivalent then of a stage curtain, of a screen, he fancied his mother crying, begging "there isn't a dime in the house," his father turning over in bed, mute in powerless furor, he heard his irritated sighs along with the groans from the mattress. It was during *the crisis*, the years 1934-35 in Paris, his father had lost his job. He heard his heart beat in his ears. Memory screen? (But with Freud one proceeds no further than screens in any case: everything is a screen if one supposes an origin. *Sup-po-sition* is already production of appearance, theater). In any case: musical experience and experimental music, without success, without failure, but with *event*: event that in one swoop clears away libidinal economy, political economy and the economy of sound.

Freud tells the hysteric: you are seeing things, you are fantasizing, tell me what you see, as you tell me about it, the consistency of the images will melt away. So there is a theater of images, of which the hysteric is the spectator, on the couch. Upon this, Freud constructs a second set-up where the hysteric is an actress, and the analyst, the invisible listener; radio comes after theater, more precisely, a radio hooked up to the auditorium, the listener not seeing the stage himself, as in radio commentary of boxing matches, football games. The charges invested in images will be *spent*, but in words. These words (the patient's, the commentator's) will butt against the analyst's silence: energizing silence, of course—these words given as a request for love will remain unanswered. If the analyst were to reply, it would be as if he himself had stepped out onto the stage. Far from dissolving the phantasy, this would reinforce it, which is what happens in everyday ordinary life, where the hysteric has eyes and does not hear. But here, in Doctor Freud's office, what is keeping silent in and being kept silent by the phantastic mise-en-scène must be heard. The analyst's silence *must* put an end (?) to the silence of the hysteric. Obliteration of the operations of production in the symptom, exhibition of these same operations in the analysis: two silences with inverse functions; the silence of noise, of the imaginary, the silence of structure, of the symbolical; and like a springboard from one to the other, the silence of the analyst. All three the complementary elements of a single device, that of analysis. The words the patient addresses to the analyst carry the murmur of the affects; they meet with the doctor's silence, thanks to which they will be distributed throughout the "pure" silence of *ratio*, which separates distinctive units (phonemes) and allows us to recognize the verbal signifier and to communicate. This is why the scene described to the analyst under these conditions will be "freed," put back into circulation, liquidated, "redeemed," says Freud. The phantom-phantasy that shackled it will be removed; the true God, Logos, will triumph.

They say that there is no music in Freud. As a theme, none indeed; but as disposition, there is as much of it as in *Exodus*, which incites us to mark his parentage with Schönberg. The hysterics are the people of Israel, who desire signs (answers) and idols, and who dance and sing around the golden calf: for Freud, this is Strauss, the Italians, Catholics (Wagner, women?). Jehovah, for his part, does not sing and is not singable: according to a short text on Hebrew vowels and the unpronounceability of the tetragram, to be able to *voice* the name of the father would be to bestow upon him a sensible, sensuous, idolatrous presence. Tonal music belongs to the stage of phantasy. (See the text concerning the phantasy of the small rhythmic sound whose stage director Freud supposes to be clitoral masturbation.) Aron, the weak one, is an adorable tenor, to whom has been parcelled out melody and the *espressivo*. As for Moses, he speaks on the near side of song without singing, speaks in modulations, as though Schönberg had invented *Sprechgesang* just for him; Schönberg's libretto is the least equivocal there is, beginning with: *Einziger, ewiger allgegenwärtiger, unsichtbarer und unvorstellbarer Gott* (act I, scene I). The music of the cure apparatus is that of the opera *Moses und Aron*. Unfinished work, interminable analysis. Like Judaism, analysis—notably of the Lacanian kind—lays down a principle that the noise-silence of the passions *must* be dissipated by the silence of the Signifier. By way of a reversal isomorphic to that of Judaism, analysis calls Signifier not the given, as is the case in linguistics, the side of the sign perceived by the speakers, but the "subject," assumed to be the producer of the *system* of signs. Not the words of Moses and Aron, but the silence *of* Jehovah = the silence that he observes (no answer), and the silence he has others observe (unpronounceable). In this set-up, the analyst is the commutator (itself silent) of one silence into another, like Moses.

Sprechgesang is passage from the melodic silence of the passions to systematic, combinatory silence; this passage is supported by the silence of the father.

Schönberg is the Luther of new music, serialism was his Reformed Church; just as Deleuze and Guattari say that Freud was the Luther of the unconscious; just as Engels says that Adam Smith was the Luther of modern political economy. Religion is *critiqued* within the confines of silence, and psychiatry within the confines of therapeutics, political economy within the confines of private property. These confines are the boundaries of the temple or the museum (concert hall), or the notary's study, or the office: limits #1, those of the building. The Reformation is only the destruction of limits #2, those that inside the building, in the theatrical (religious-political-musical-pictorial) apparatus called "Italian-style," separate the auditorium from the stage: the proscenium arch, the dais for the chief, the rostrum for the orator, the picture frame: boundaries that hypothetically cannot be crossed without the donning of a disguise. Hidden behind limits #2 are the true limits #3, the effaced operators of effacement, of mise-en-scène, of harmony and composition, or rhetoric and power, of the so-called legitimate construction. Schönberg, as Adorno rightly points out, wants to destroy appearances; Schönberg's exodus is far from musical Egypt, from continuous Wagnerian modulation, from expressionism, from *musica ficta*, in the direction of the desert: voluntary impoverishment of means, the series, the two operations–inversion and retrogradation, the four positions—a, a', $\overline{a}$, $\overline{a}'$. This parsimony, by its very rigor, will make it possible to confront dissonances in all their consequences:

> I wanted to reach those who seek their personal salvation on the road of the golden mean. For that is the only road that does not lead to Rome [=*to the promised Land*]. Those people follow that route, who, gluttons, glean dissonances, wanting to pass for moderns, but [who] do not have the audacity to suffer the consequences, which result not only from the disso-

nances themselves, but also, and much more so, from
the consonances that preceded them. (Preface to *Three
Satires*, 1925)

To extend the principle of dissonance universally is *to stop
misleading the ear*: the principle of *immobilization*, the same one
that Cézanne's eye obeyed twenty-five years earlier in the Aix
landscape and the one by means of which this Moses of new
painting also wanted to stop misleading the eye. Now one will stay
in place, there will be no resolution in the vanishing point, where
the multiple gathers itself together, there will be no history, no
salutary epiphany, there is a language without intention that
requires not religion but faith. Schönberg criticizes music as an
edifying recital, he wants to turn it into a *discourse*, produced by a
language that is an arbitrary system, yet developed in all of its
consequences (the language of Jehovah) and thus always
experienced as unacceptable and tragic: something like the
unconscious according to Lacan. A new transcendence is
introduced into sound material, all familiarity becomes impossible,
the tragic triumphs, as in Freud. What the dodecaphonic and serial
"technique," as well as analysis, seek is the tragic, which in
Freud's as in Schönberg's view is entirely lacking in the scientific
or musical positivism of the nineteenth century. The tragic is
intensity divested of signification, yet ascribed to the intention of
an Other.

The return of Judaism as the device underlying both works
has indeed a critical function in relation to a-critical society and
ideology, as Adorno says of Schönberg, but probably not where
Adorno expected it. The desensitization of the material cannot be
attributed to industrial society and its techniques of mechanical
reproduction (which, as we know, can just as well produce the
opposite, i.e., hypersensitization; just listen to the music of Kagel,
Cage, Xenakis, Zappa, Hendrix). Neither can the Benjaminian
concept of the destruction of the *aura*, which also belongs to the
negative thinking of the lost *chef d'oeuvre*, of modern technology
as alienation, be of any use to us here. The desensitization in

Schönberg or Lacan arises from the image of *therapeutics*, which haunts Schönberg's work as much as it does Freud's: therapeutics through a reinforcement of discourse, discontinuity, rationality, law, silence-law, negativity, not at all in the spirit of positivism but in that of tragic negativism, fate, the unconscious, dispossession. Freudian and post-Freudian works teach us what this tragic negativism consists in: the mapping back of the cure apparatus, controlled transference, onto the primary process: reconstituting a critical theater in the doctor's office (after dismissal of the supposedly pre-critical theater of the parental chambers and the visual phantasy); blocking out the vertiginous discovery of libidinal displaceability of primary work, nomadism. And this mapping back, this restoration, go unrecognized by Freud himself, *ignored* in their arbitrary nature, in their unjustifiable madness as *device*, as figure of the unconscious, of *psychoanalysis itself* [ignored and suspected: reread the end of the analysis of Senatspräsident Schreber where Freud writes essentially this: nothing resembles more my own theory of drives and libidinal investments than that of Schreberian rays, but all the same I found it first and I have witnesses! Is there more true theory in his delusion or more delusion in my theory? The future will tell. . . And again in *Moses and Monotheism*, the ultimate text, that in its entirety deals with the question: what is the madness proper (the device proper) that is Judaism?]

There was a time, the period of *Human, All Too Human*, when Nietzsche desired this tragic, intellectual, anti-Wagnerian, sober, critical, Voltairian-Pauline-Mosaic music, period of convalescence, period of non-affirmation, period that was, in sum, both sickly and healthy, like "the times." But when Nietzsche strides over "the times" to occupy his untimely anachronism, it is no longer criticism he needs or nihilism, even true nihilism, or the Judaism that he, too, loved so much, but the affirmative, the music of Cage.

Though his experience was space-time, writes Cage of Schönberg, *his idea of unity was two-dimensional: vertical and horizontal. On paper.* The "idea" is not only technical, a chordal technique that reworks segments of the horizontal series vertically: this idea is the predominance of the written, the law, which destroys illusion: no apparent surface on which to inscribe a text, because no effect of depth, no background. Instead of idols, the Torah, a discourse without a third dimension. Is it by chance that Cage's remark immediately follows this one: *he was depressed by criticism because there were no limitations to his sense of responsibility.* These abolished limitations, are limits #2 and #3; this responsibility is the power for you to be seized by the words addressed to you, even before you have heard what they say, explains Levinas.

It took the complete development of serial "poverty" after World War II in order for us to perceive the poverty without the quotation marks, outlined candidly here: after the first steps in the twelve-tone method (1914-1915, a symphony whose final portion was taken up again in *Jacob's Ladder*, itself unfinished), "I was continually preoccupied," writes Schönberg, "with the intention of grounding the structure of my music consciously on a unifying idea that would produce not only all the other ideas but also regulate their accompaniment and the chords, the 'harmonies'." (1937) By which it is clearly understood that this musical device, to the extent that it is a system of exclusions and connections of sound flows, remains analogous to the system of tonal music: Bach must have said something of the sort concerning the *Musical Offering*. Schönberg has indeed destroyed limits #2 and #3, but not limits #1. Satire is a literary theatrical genre, the Hebrew religion a religion, political criticism a politics. No longer is there resolution into surface chords, no more appearance, but there is a reserve in the silence of composition; like the analyst, the composer is on the side of the signifier. But it is not enough to display limits #2 and #3, as does Brecht, in order to be over and done with representation as ideology and phantasy. The tragic is also a libidinal device. Theatricality reconstitutes itself with the tragic. The vertiginous dissonance becomes melodic. Psychoanalysis has carried out the critique of domination Italian-style, Egyptian-style, visual domination, the domination of phantasy, but from within a space that is still a space of Lutheran, Hebrew, auditory, sober domination. What is needed is a "practice" (a word probably devoid of meaning as soon as it no longer refers to a "subject"), a practice that is not dominated, without domain, without *domus*, without the cupola of the Duomo of Florence in Brunelleschi's little box, but also the vessel of the Ark of the Covenant that contains the stone tablets. Without arche: and even without *an-arche*, Daniel Charles! To interpret Cage with Levinas, or even Heidegger, is to persevere within nihilism.

When Cage says: there is no silence, he says: no Other holds dominion over sound, there is no God, no Signifier as principle of unification or composition. There is no filtering, no set blank spaces, no exclusions; neither is there a work anymore, no more limits #1 to determine musicality as a region. We make music all the time, "no sooner finish one than begin making another just as people keep on washing dishes, brushing their teeth, getting sleepy and so on: *noise, noise, noise.* The wisest thing to do is to open one's ears immediately, and hear a sound suddenly be-fore one's thinking has a chance to turn into something logical, abstract, or symbolical." (*A Year From Monday*, "Julliard Lecture") Thus, liquidate, liquify limit #1, the element that selects what is musical, that results in there being thus-and-so sounds to listen to and thus-and-so ears capable of listening to them (these ears can, for example—and it's a sign of their capacities—treat themselves to seats, good seats, the seats of princes, inside a concert hall). To destroy limit #1 is to establish all noise as sound, body noise, the unheard-of noises of the social "body." Silence is displaced: it is no longer the composer's, the signifier's, Jehovah's silence that must remain unheard, be effaced, but silence as noise-sound of the involuntary body, the noise-sound of the libido wandering over bodies, "nature," that must be heard.

A critical political party also inhabits the silence of the signifier, the silence of domination; it considers the surface of experience as appearance, mere symptom, and even if it decides not to take power, power is already taken by it to the extent that it repeats this device of appearance and effacement, of theater, of politics as a *domaine*. Even should "tonal resolution" be deferred endlessly, this party will be a tragic political party, it will be the negative dialectic of the *Aufklarung*; it is the Frankfurt School, demythologized, Lutheran, nihilistic Marxism.

The answer is not *spontaneism*: for "sounds are not men," says Cage, libidinal flows are not men, freedom is not *someone's* freedom, activity is not *expression*. *Spontaneism* still maps energetic commutations back onto a memory, a subject, an identity. It still belongs to theatricality (the "nature" it invokes is the sole subject of Western theater: its "outside"). I don't know what the answer is. The question is: what is the silence of *kapital*, its silence as a composer and stage director? First answer: it is the law of value, the single rule, i.e. the exchangeability of equal quantities (of labor?). Now, this law allows, encourages dissonances: the most diverse objects (sonorous and other) find their rate of exchange in this composition as long as they are exchangeable (sale-able). No need for us to cry over that, we do not want more order, a music that is more tonal, more unified, or more rich and elegant. We want less order, more circulation by chance, by free wandering: the abolition of the law of value, which constitutes the body of *kapital* as a surface to puncture, as appearance. Second answer: Daniel Buren writes concerning *Documenta 5* (Kassel, 1972), "More and more the subject of an exhibition tends not to be the exhibition of works of art, but the exhibition of the exhibition as a work of art (...). The work today serves only as a decorative gadget for the survival of the Museum as painting, painting whose author is none other than the organizer of the exhibition himself." Transposed to *Kapital*: it is *produktion* no longer of products, but of productions; *konsumption* no longer of objects, but of consumptions; *musikke* no longer of sounds, but of musics. So that the question is: the silence heard in noise, *immediately, suddenly*, is it not still dominated by the unheard silence of the Komposer-organizer, capital? *Kapital*, is it not the stage director of noises and silences themselves, as mise-en-scène? Destroy the work, but also destroy the work of works and *non-works*, kapitalism as museum, as memory of everything that is possible. De-memorize, like the unconscious.

Translated by Joseph Maier

Notes on the Texts

"Dérives," a text dated October 1972, was first published as the introduction to *Dérive à partir de Marx et Freud* (Union Générale d'Éditions, 10/18, 1973). This is the first publication in English.

"Sur la théorie" was first published in *VH 101* magazine in the summer of 1970. This is the first publication in English.

"Oedipe juif" first appeared in *Critique,* 277, June 1970. The English translation (revised here) was initially published by *Genre,* 10, (1977), pp. 395-411.

"Convivences du désir avec le figural" was first published as a section of *Discours, figure,* Lyotard's doctoral thesis (Éditions Klincksieck, 1971).

"Notes sur la fonction critique de l'oeuvre" was first published in the *Revue de'esthétique* (XXIII, 3, & 4, December 1970). This is the first publication in English.

"La Dent, la paume" a text dated September 1972, was first published in *Des dispositifs pulsionnels* (Union Générale d'Éditions, 10/18, 1973). This translation, revised here, appeared first in *Substance,* 15, 1977, pp. 105-10.

"Plusiers silences" first appeared in *Musique en jeu,* 9, November 1972. This is the first publication in English.

Biographical Note

Born in Versailles in 1924, Jean-Francois Lyotard studied literature and philosophy. He taught and was involved in trade-unionism in Algeria from 1950 to 1952. He militated within the group *Pouvoir ouvrier,* wrote for *Socialisme ou barbarie,* and was a member of the latter's Editorial Board from 1956 to 1964. He supported the Algerian liberation movement and took an active part in the events of May 1968 in France. A former lecturer at the Sorbonne and the University of Nanterre (Paris X), he earned his Ph.D in 1971. He currently teaches both within the Department of Philosophy and at the *Institut polytechnique de philosophie* of the University of Vincennes (Paris VIII). The roving professor, who also teaches abroad, has been the guest of Johns Hopkins University, Baltimore, the University of California at San Diego, the Center for XXth Century Studies in Milwaukee, the University of Montreal and the University of Sao Paulo, among other institutions of higher learning.

Uncollected Works ★

1954 *La phénoménologie*, P.U.F., Que sais-je? 8th printing: 1976.

1971 *Discours, figure*, Klincksieck, Collection d'esthétique; 3rd printing: 1977.

1973 *Drive a partir de Marx et Freud*, Union générale d'éditions (10/18) 2nd printing: 1975.

1973 *Des dispositifs pulsionnels*, Union générale d'éditions (10/18); 2nd printing (Bourgois): 1979.

1974 *Economie Libidinale*, Minuit, Critique.

1977 *Instructions païennes*, Galilée, Débats.

1977 *Rudiments païen, genre dissertatif*, Union générale d'éditions (10/18).

1977 *Les transformateurs Duchamp*. Galilée (Ecritures/figures).

1977 *Récits tremblants*, (in collaboration with Jacques Monory), Galilée (Ecritures/figures).

1979 *La condition postmoderne*, rapport sur le savoir, Minuit, Critique

1979 *Au juste* (conversations with J.-L. Thébaub), Christian Bourgois.

1979 *Le mur du Pacifique*, narrative, Galilée (Ligne fictive).

★ Including only books published in French. Jean-Francois Lyotard's articles and translations of his works into various languages, as well as articles concerning him, are too numerous to be mentioned here. An extremely useful source of information in this regard, one should note however, is the special issue of the review *l'Arc* (No. 64, 1976), entirely devoted to Lyotard.

Translators

Susan Hanson has studied with J.-F. Lyotard in Paris and at the Johns Hopkins University, were she wrote her dissertation on Nathalie Sarraute and the politics of suspicion.

Richard Lockwood completed a Ph.D. in Romance languages at the Johns Hopkins University in 1982. His thesis examines the rhetorical pragmatics of speeches by Racine and Bossuet. He has worked with J.-F. Lyotard on several topics, notably Plato's critique and practice of rhetoric.

Joseph Maier studied at Northwestern University, at the University of Paris-Vincennes and at the Johns Hopkins University; he was a student of J.-F. Lyotard, among others, at both of the latter. he was a student of J.-F. Lyotard, among others, at both of the latter. He is currently assistant editor/translation editor with the Population Information Program of the Johns Hopkins University.

Ann Matejka has studied in Belgium, the USA and France. She is currently working on a doctorate at the Ecole des hautes études en sciences sociales, Paris.

Roger McKeon studied philosophy with J.-F. Lyotard at the University of Paris (Nanterre) from 1967 to 1969. He works as a translator with the United Nations.